Central and Local Government Relations

Central and Local Government Relations

A Comparative Analysis of
West European Unitary States

edited by
Edward C. Page and
Michael J. Goldsmith

Ⓢ SAGE Modern Politics Series Volume 13
Sponsored by the European Consortium for
Political Research/ECPR

Ⓢ SAGE Publications
London • Newbury Park • Beverly Hills • New Delhi

SAGE Publications Ltd
28 Banner Street
London EC1Y 8QE

 SAGE Publications Inc
275 South Beverly Drive
Beverly Hills, California 90212
SAGE Publications Inc
2111 West Hillcrest Street
Newbury Park, California 91320

SAGE Publications India Pvt Ltd
C-236 Defence Colony
New Delhi 110 024

British Library Cataloguing in Publication Data

Central and local government relations:
    a comparative analysis of West European
    unitary states. — (Sage studies in modern
    politics; 13).
    1. Local government — Europe
    I. Page, Edward   II. Goldsmith, Michael
    352.04   JS3000.2

ISBN 0-8039-8071-X

Library of Congress catalog card number 87-061112

Printed in Great Britain by J.W. Arrowsmith Ltd, Bristol

Contents

Preface

This book examines variations in the relationship between central and local government in seven unitary countries of West Europe. It is the first attempt to make such a systematic comparison across countries, and we hope others will be able to build on the foundations laid here. In undertaking the project, we were conscious of the fact that, although there are many excellent studies of local government and intergovernmental relations in a variety of countries, there have been few attempts at a systematic comparison of the kind necessary to achieve the kind of understanding we believe to be desirable. We were also aware that, by ourselves, we lacked sufficient knowledge of other countries to undertake the kind of comparative analysis we wanted. To achieve that objective, it was clear that we needed the collaboration of colleagues in other countries.

The European Consortium for Political Research (ECPR) came to our help by inviting a small group of collaborators to its research sessions in Trento, Italy, of September 1983. Together, we developed a research proposal that was subsequently funded by the British Economic and Social Research Council under grant no. E002322089. This funding not only enabled the group to meet at the ECPR's 1984 and 1985 research sessions in Florence and Umea, Sweden, but also allowed us some limited research assistance to collect essential comparative data, a task willingly and expertly undertaken by Tom Clegg.

Systematic comparison depends on the analytic framework used and the quality of the comparative data available. The framework developed here and set out in Chapter 1 is based on the simple fact that local government performs different functions in different countries, with varying levels of discretion in the way it performs those functions, and of access to upper tiers of government in order to influence policy and service decisions. This is especially true when the details of particular subfunctions are examined, and when the different ways in which discretion may be exercised or curtailed are considered. These differences raise problems for comparative analysis. Our early group meetings were used to overcome some of these difficulties, through the development of a common analytical framework and agreement on the data sought. Furthermore, the quality and quantity of local government data — although variable — are generally good, and the group took every effort to standardize the data collected.

Our choice of countries was limited to seven unitary states: Denmark, France, Great Britain, Italy, Norway, Spain and Sweden. The decision to limit the study to unitary states was tactical rather than theoretical, allowing us to avoid the additional complications that would accrue from the inclusion of federal systems. But we believe there is no reason why our analytic framework should not be applied to federal systems; indeed, colleagues from the United States, Canada and West Germany have all indicated that it has relevance to an understanding of local government and intergovernmental relations in those countries. Even the choice of unitary countries poses the problem of defining a unitary state, and more specifically whether Spain and Italy (and maybe even France) are still unitary in structure. Given our decision to choose unitary states for tactical rather than theoretical reasons, we do not believe the enterprise stands or falls on the contentious issue of whether or not these countries remain unitary. Last, but not necessarily least, our choice of countries reflected the fact that a considerable body of research has been conducted on central–local government relations in the chosen seven.

Building on these foundations, we review the status of local government in each country in terms of the functions it performs, the discretion it has in performing those functions, and the access it has to central government. Using the common framework and data requirements, each contributor was asked to examine a particular country, but was left free to determine what he saw as the most important features and trends in its intergovernmental relations. In a concluding chapter, we compare the situation across the countries considered, drawing a distinction between the North European group — Scandinavia and Britain — and the South European countries — France, Germany and Spain — and outline a range of possible explanations for the differences found.

This book thus provides a picture of intergovernmental relations in our chosen countries and suggests explanations for them. In a later work, the group hopes to explore the common themes uncovered and to consider more extensively the theoretical explanations for them.

In carrying out this project we have incurred many debts. Ken Newton encouraged us throughout the enterprise, and Jeanette Becquart-Leclercq participated in the early discussions on the project. Jack Hayward offered useful comments on early drafts; Valerie Stewart helped us to organize our group meetings. Colleagues and graduate students at the London School of Economics provided valuable comments on our ideas when presented to George Jones's comparative local government seminar. Pat Bellotti typed the manuscript in her usual capable fashion. We are most grateful to all of them, but remain, as is the custom, responsible for what follows. Page and Goldsmith shared the editorial burden in that order — a burden made more tolerable by the musical support of Miles, Monk and Mingus.

Ed Page
Mike Goldsmith
Hull/Salford, December 1986

1

Centre and locality: functions, access and discretion

Edward C. Page and Michael J. Goldsmith

In the postwar period, the study of local government in West European countries has been dominated by two concerns, both of which have received a major impetus from the practical policy concerns of government. The first is the question of reorganization, expressed in terms of how 'best' to organize local government units to provide public services — whether or not the criteria of 'best' involves narrowly technical or more widely political factors (Sharpe, 1978; Dearlove, 1979). In the 1960s and 1970s, governments brought forward proposals to change the size of local government units; some of these proposals were fully implemented, as in Britain and the Scandinavian countries, but in other states, such as Italy and France, the implementation was more patchy. They also brought forward proposals to change patterns of management, such as corporate management structures, and financial and policy planning systems. Over time, quite a large body of academic literature associated with establishing the need for such changes — and the impact of any changes made — was produced (reviewed, for example, in Rowat, 1980).

The second concern is related, but in some senses even more basic. This is the question of decentralization: what should be the powers and capabilities of local government in modern states? Since the onset of the fiscal squeeze on local government in the mid-1970s, central government policies aimed at reducing the level of grants to local government and, more generally, local expenditure in some countries, such as Britain and Norway, have led to a perceived centralization of government; in other states, such as Italy and France, measures aimed at decentralization have been introduced as part of a commitment by central government to restructure processes of decision making and increase the role of local government within them.

Within this field of decentralization, three major academic concerns have developed. First has been a concern with documenting the precise nature of the system of decentralization as far as local government is concerned; how much of the action in policy making goes on at the local level, or involves local political and administrative elites? Of course, the classic studies of these questions, such as Griffith (1966) for Britain and Worms (1966) for France, predated the fiscal squeeze, and recent debates about further centralization or decentralization. However, their work provides the inspiration for a number of studies describing patterns of central–local government relations in different countries. Second, there has been a concern with establishing the precise nature and significance of any changes in central–local relations; how far have reforms introduced or proposed changed patterns of such relations? For example, there is a body of literature in France, Spain and Italy that looks at the importance of regionalization as a factor altering traditional patterns of central–local relations (Mény, 1982), and in Britain that studies the impact of the restrictions on local spending imposed by the 1979 Conservative government on more traditional conceptions of what local autonomy should involve (Goldsmith and Newton, 1984). Third, there has been a concern with explaining patterns of central–local relations: what they are, and why they are being changed? For example, such patterns may result from the inherent nature of urban services, as suggested by the 'dual state' thesis (Saunders, 1984), or from the national culture of political parties (Becquart-Leclercq, 1976; Bulpitt, 1983). Changes in central–local relations may result from the 'fiscal crisis' of modern states (Boddy, 1984), or from longstanding ideological commitments to decentralization found within political parties.

Each of these three questions — the nature of the existing system, the type and direction of change, and the causes of different patterns and changes — is inherently comparative. For the first two, describing salient patterns and their changes, we need a conceptualization of how things would be different if the factors deemed important were absent. Such comparisons may take the form (frequently implicitly) of a counterfactual hypothesis (concerning what the system would look like without the doctrine of *ultra vires* or the *cumul des mandats*), or of a comparison with another organization within the state, such as a quango or health service institution. Alternatively, the comparison may be crossnational. Crossnational comparison is only one, albeit important, strategy for picking out the salient features of central–local relations in any one country. Such explanations that do exist typically refer to broad socioeconomic and political forces shaping local government structures and relationships that are in principle applicable and testable in the context of a crossnational comparison. Any convincing explanation for the emergence of a particular pattern of central–local government relations in one country must be able to explain why identical patterns are or are not found in others.

But before we can describe and explain differences in patterns of central–local government relations, we need to determine what salient features should be described and explained. It is trite but true to say that most studies of central –local relations are concerned with the extent to which local government units can shape the way in which the benefits and sanctions of modern government are provided to its citizens. Where local influence is extensive, government is often argued to be more decentralized than where its influence is more limited. Indeed, it is conventional for crossnational descriptions to use terms such as 'centralization', 'decentralization', 'central control' and 'local autonomy'. These terms are certainly useful in a large number of contexts, yet they do not on their own provide adequate concepts on which to base a comparative analysis. It could be claimed, with some justification, that France's system is more centralized than Britain's on the grounds that local government in France does rather little; however, it could also be claimed, with equal justification, that Britain is the more centralized because local political opposition to central government proposals in France is far more potent and effective than it is in Britain, as was seen during the process of local government reorganization in the 1960s and 1970s (Ashford, 1982).

The problem with such terms is not that they are wrong, but rather that they do not clarify what particular aspect of the process of government is 'decentralized'. Consequently, when such terms are employed, it is relatively easy for studies of central –local government relations in different countries to talk past one another. In order to make valid comparisons, it is necessary to have a framework for comparison that removes the ambiguity in existing terminology, yet remains relatively comprehensive by accounting for the variety of different aspects of central –local relations, the importance of which has already been demonstrated in a number of single and two-country comparisons.

It is possible to distinguish three broad dimensions that may be used to evaluate the position of local government institutions in the modern state; the functions, access and discretion of local authorities. In this book, the authors offer a description of central –local relations in seven unitary countries of West Europe — Britain, Denmark, France, Italy, Norway, Spain, Sweden — on these three dimensions. European states have been taken as the focus because they share a common heritage and experience as far as local government is concerned (Hintze, 1962). Unitary countries have been chosen because, at this early stage in the generation of comparative description and theory of local –central government relations, the federal structure introduces a degree of complexity that we do not wish to confront.

Why are the three dimensions of functions, access and discretion important as a means of structuring our analysis? There are two main reasons. First, in terms of describing the scope for local influence in state service provision they offer a logical approach to the three forms which that influence might take, although the precise mechanisms through which local influence is exerted under these headings are multiple. The role that local government plays in shaping state services is a function of the tasks it has to carry out — how far it can make its own decisions about how to carry out these tasks and how far it can shape key processes of decision making in the centre. These processes not only define local tasks and the discretion allowed local authorities, but also allocate key resources, such as money and legal authorization, to enable them to carry out their functions. Moreover, as will be shown later, the threefold division corresponds to latent distinctions present in much of the literature on central–local relations. Second, this division suggests that different bodies of political science literature should be explored in order to explain the three dimensions of central–local relations.

**Functions, access, discretion and local influence
in modern political systems**
There is an obvious variation in the importance of local government as a provider of services crossnationally; in some systems, it has more functions than others. In some countries, such as New Zealand, local government does very little and can therefore make little overall impact on the nature of public services; in others, such as Denmark, a wide range of services, including income maintenance, is part of local government's responsibility (Bowman and Hampton, 1983; Skovsgaard, 1984). In the Scandinavian countries, a large number of crucial public services are in the hands of local government, including health care, but not the police services: the reverse applies in Britain. The ability to shape state benefits and sanctions is, ceteris paribus, more extensive where the range of services fulfilled by local government is broader. Variation in the range of functions, can, of course, be found within a single country, as in the United States, where the diversity of local government structures and functions represents an embarrassment of riches; within the UK, the functions of local government in Northern Ireland differ greatly from those elsewhere (Birrell and Murie, 1980).

It is important to be cautious in comparing the functions of local government crossnationally for two main reasons. First, services vary in terms of their nature, mode of delivery and nominal description. For example, public housing aid in France consists primarily of cheap loans to housing agencies (HLM — Habitation à loyer moderé) rather than direct public subsidy to the council rental sector, as in Britain. In France, franchises issued by the local authority to private companies are frequently used to deliver services such as refuse collection and disposal, as opposed to the direct labour or contracting-out arrangements common in Britain and Scandinavia. Terms used to describe public services crossnationally may refer to different activities: for example, industrial development in Britain refers primarily to promotion through publicity, whereas in Italy and Spain local government authorities have far more extensive powers to offer cheap loans and subsidies. The second reason for caution in comparing functions crossnationally derives from the fact that the way functions are allocated varies crossnationally. In Spain, Italy and France, there is relatively little for which local government has exclusive responsibility, with central ministries having direct or directive control over some services, while in Britain and the Scandinavian countries central ministries have little to do with the execution of policies. For example, in education French and Italian communes have some school building and maintenance functions, but no exclusive right to determine the location of schools or maintenance standards.

For local government to 'have' or 'fulfil' a service, or part of it, means little more than that local authorities have formal responsibility for employing people to carry it out. It does not necessarily mean that they can influence the way in which it is carried out because they may have little discretion to do so. For example, local authorities in Britain have responsibility for administering income maintenance payments in the form of housing benefits, yet at most they can influence the distribution of these benefits only in a marginal way, since they are administered according to national regulations (Erskine, 1984). As a result, it is not sufficient to look at what local government does. Although the scale of local government responsibilities, relative to those of the central state, is a much-loved indicator of centralization and decentralization among some economists and political scientists (King, 1984; Ashford, 1979), it is clearly inadequate since the ability to make significant decisions affecting a function is not identical with formal responsibility for it.

In order to examine the degree to which local government can shape the services of the modern state, it is necessary to go beyond an examination of its formal responsibilities to look at the degree of discretion that it has in carrying out these functions. Discretion refers to the ability of actors within local government to make decisions about the type and level of services it delivers within the formal statutory and administrative framework for local service delivery, and about how that service is provided and financed. There are at least four possible components of this type of discretion.

First, discretion may be significantly related to the general legal framework of local government. In particular, there is a distinction, discussed by Smith (1985:87), between those countries — including Scandinavia — where there is a supposition that local authorities have a general competence to undertake services, and those where local government is obliged to find some form of specific statutory basis for its actions, as implied in the doctrine of ultra vires in Britain. Another possible general legal principle is that of the concentration of the powers of tutelage in the hands of a set of central officials responsible for one of a defined set of local government authorities, as with the case of the prefect in France before 1982, which contrasts with the absence of a formal holder of tutelage powers in Britain, and the importance of special administrative courts and complaints procedures that may delimit local government powers in the Scandinavian countries.

Second, an overall evaluation of the discretion of local government may be a function of the degree of discretion that local government authorities have in a number of particular local services. For example, this might distinguish between mandated services, such as education in Britain and Scandinavia, or school building in France and Italy, and those based on a broad grant of permissive power, including leisure and cultural services in most countries. Perhaps more important, the discretion within any one service may be constrained by detailed, centrally specified standards of service provision (for example, income maintenance in Britain and Scandinavia), or the standards of service may be so loosely defined that they impose almost no constraints on local government actions (for example, consumer protection officials in Britain have to enforce national regulations, but they do so in a locally variable manner).

Third, local government discretion may be constrained by non-legal forms of influence; in some countries, government advice — often in the form of circulars — may enjoy such a status that it becomes a surrogate for legal forms of influence. This may be because central advice is deemed worthy of note because it embodies the superior technical expertise found within the centre, because it takes on the force of law through being accepted as a binding interpretation of the law, or because potential non-compliance is discouraged through threats of legal or financial penalties. Compliance through ascription of superior expertise is especially important because it offers greater possibilities for routine influence without overt challenges through the courts or outright defiance. In some polities, such as Britain, local government professionals have acquired a relatively high status as a source of expert advice. In areas such as roads and public transport, local expertise has been influential in shaping central policy, although in others, such as housing and leisure, it has been less important (see

Dunleavy, 1981a; 1981b; Goldsmith, 1983). In France, on the other hand, central state bureaucrats still lay claim to a monopoly of expertise, especially in areas of technical service dominated by the Grands Corps of the *Ponts et Chaussees* (Thoenig, 1973).

Fourth, local government discretion may reflect its financial discretion. Central government decisions in all European states account for a large portion of local income, in the form of grants or assigned revenues. In some countries, such as the Netherlands, central government determines almost exclusively the level of local government income, while in others there exists a greater or lesser degree of discretion in raising revenue locally. An examination of financial discretion would include a description of the degree to which the tax system, including tax bases and tax rates, and capital and current spending levels, as well as local fees and charges, are shaped by central government decisions. It might also include the degree to which spending on particular services is constrained because grants are earmarked in specific and conditional form, as opposed to being general revenue-sharing grants-in-aid to no specific service.

The access of local government refers to the nature of contacts between central and local government actors. Local government may have limited discretion, being subject to central constraints in the form of laws, advice, grants and so on. However, if local actors themselves have a significant influence on central decisions, they have greater scope for shaping state services than if central decisions were simply the product of an interaction between non-local politicians, bureaucrats and groups — which typifies much of central policy making in western countries (Richardson, 1982) — that excluded them.

In some countries, such as Italy and France, contact between central and local government is frequently conducted on the basis of face-to-face meetings between individual members of local authorities, and politicians and officials in the central state. In France, this form of face-to-face contact is further supported (but not, of course, necessarily caused) by the *cumul des mandats*, the accumulation of offices through which the mayors of predominantly large towns acquire national office and use this to bring benefits to their own communes. This face-to-face contact contrasts with the position in Britain, where contacts between central and local government actors are largely indirect (Griffith, 1966), with the national associations of elected councillors and non-elected officials constituting the major channels through which central government maintains contact on issues that go beyond statutory approval for individual capital proposals.

There are two broad and inter-related questions to be explored in the context of patterns of access between central and local government actors. First, how frequent and important are direct forms of access in comparison with indirect forms? Second, do these patterns of access give local government actors privileged access to central government decision-making processes? The answer to the first question tells us something about the nature of local influence within the centre: indirect forms of access are unlikely to be able to express the preferences of individual local government authorities. What gets taken up with the centre are the issues on which there is sufficient agreement within the national associations through which indirect patterns of access are channelled. For an individual local authority, this offers less scope for influence on matters that concern it more specifically, and thus the channels of access to some extent constrain the types of issues on which local government can influence the centre. The answer to the second question relates directly to the central concern of the comparative analysis: it determines how far central government actors are likely to pay attention to the views and representations of local government actors, whether channelled through direct or indirect forms of access. On the basis of American and French experience (Haider, 1974; Becquart-Leclercq, 1976), one would expect direct forms of access to offer greater scope for privileged forms of access, not least because the national interest group arena is highly competitive. Local government associations of elected representatives are not as specialized as other functionally specific groups, and their expertise is likely to be shared, if not overshadowed, by that of others, frequently those of professional associations such as finance officers, planners, architects or lawyers (see Dunleavy, 1981a; 1981b). Consequently, one would expect the broad, non-function-specific local authority association to be at a disadvantage relative to other functionally based interest groups.

The use of the framework
We have set out the categories of functions, access and discretion as a means of distinguishing three main ways in which local government can influence state service delivery, and outlined a number of possible variations along these three dimensions. Yet what is the advantage in making such distinctions between functions, access and discretion? The first has already been alluded to; they facilitate a more adequate comparative description of relationships between central and local government crossnationally than is possible under the simple use of terms such as 'centralization' and 'decentralization', or terms designed for two-country comparisons, such as 'dogmatism' and 'pragmatism', but inapplicable much beyond them (Ashford, 1982). The three dimensions used here allow one to look for salient

differences in central–local government relations with greater precision than is possible using existing terminology, and to avoid the problem of analyses of different countries concentrating on different features of the relationship and therefore talking past one another. Comparative description, albeit on a relatively large scale, is a modest objective, yet one that has largely eluded students of central–local relations.

The framework is therefore used in this volume as a means of pinpointing differences in central–local government relations in our seven countries. The choice of countries was partly determined by the availability of information on central–local relations; Britain and France have traditionally generated a large number of such studies, and the quality of empirical research on Italy and the Scandinavian countries has been high since the mid-1960s. Spain has also generated relatively large volumes of information on central–local relations in the wake of the institutional changes since the end of the Franco regime. In addition, the seven countries lead one to expect to find a level of diversity among patterns of central–local relations sufficient to explore any theoretical approaches to explaining differences: France, Spain and Italy are each frequently characterized as 'Napoleonic' state structures, with more detailed forms of tutelary control over local government, in addition to a late development of welfare state provision (Flora and Alber, 1981:55). Britain and the Scandinavian countries have traditionally been argued to incorporate the doctrine of local self-government within their constitutions, and to have embraced the systematic provision of welfare benefits much earlier than France, Spain and Italy. Each of our contributors was asked to describe patterns of central–local relations in his country on the basis of the comparative descriptive framework.

As such, the framework does not claim to explain anything, but divides the question of the role of local government in the modern state into a useful set of dimensions. Yet the use of the framework extends beyond comparative description and may be used to facilitate explanation of these differences. Of course, explanation requires specification of the explanandum, and this is one way in which the framework may be of help. Yet the framework also suggests some of the forms that any explanation of such differences may take. Let us examine some of the possibilities suggested by the framework.

The framework suggests the possibility that different features of the three dimensions may be inter-related or, rather, that patterns of access, functions and discretion may be causally related to others. For example, direct access between national and local politicians may be associated with local government systems with less formal discretion, thanks to the tendency for actors within bureaucratic systems that attempt to regulate behaviour to exploit areas of uncertainty through use of their own powers to bargain or 'blackmail' (exercise *chantage*) those formally their superiors (Crozier, 1964). Another possible causal relationship can be hypothesized between the range of functions and levels of discretion; although the functions of local government are one dimension that helps to define its importance, paradoxically those systems in which local government does more might suffer limitations of local discretion. Where local government has extensive functional responsibilities, its actions become more important to the centre, and are therefore more likely to be the target of central influence where they affect crucial state functions, such as education or income maintenance, than where they are confined to the provision of leisure centres.

Second, the framework suggests that the explanations for differences are unlikely to be found in one existing broad general theory. Instead, the patterns of functional allocation, discretion and access appear to relate to different bodies of theory, of which not all are conventionally related directly to questions of central–local relations. For example, as far as functions are concerned two rather different types of literature spring to mind as major contenders for explaining differential patterns of functional allocation. The fiscal federalism and public choice literature (reviewed by King, 1984) has sought to establish whether certain types of services have intrinsic qualities, such as divisibility of benefits and spillover effects, which should make them a subnational function in order to optimise costs and levels of delivery. Thus one might expect some services with fewer spillovers, such as leisure and recreation, to be local rather than national. The 'dual state' thesis is based on a different set of concerns, although it too distinguishes between different types of state services; it suggests that there is an ideal typical division within the state apparatus between social investment functions (broadly operational-ized as decisions affecting capital accumulation) and social consumption functions (usually welfare-oriented policies). Social investment is a function of regional and central government, and is subject to 'corporatist' modes of interest mediation. Social consumption is a function of local government and is subject to more 'competitive' or 'pluralist' forms of interest mediation (cf. Saunders, 1984; Dunleavy, 1984).

Another set of answers to the question of functions may lie in the relationship between particular services and wider processes of political conflict within a particular country, rather than in the nature of the service per se. For example church –state conflicts historically have been at the heart of education policy in many European states, and this may, as in France, have shaped the institutional arrangements for the provision of school services (Archer, 1979).

Issues related to the discretion of local government may similarly be explored from the perspective of whether certain types of service are inherently more amenable to central direction. For example, the level of service to be delivered can better be specified quantitatively and relatively precisely in income maintenance programmes than in services where the nature of the service itself is dependent upon the discretionary judgements of the 'street level bureaucrats' (compare Kochen and Deutsch, 1980, with Lipsky, 1979; Sharpe, 1984). Alternatively, the limitations on discretion may result less from the inherent nature of the services than the broader institutional and political structure of the particular country. The historical – institutional literature, above all the work of Hintze (1962), suggests that the system of central government prefects, with direct authority over local government, is associated with political systems without a form of petty nobility equivalent to the gentry in Britain or the *Ritter* of East Elbian Prussia.

Explanations of patterns of access may take up issues raised in yet another body of literature, above all on political mobilization and nation building (Rokkan, 1970), exploring the degree to which local political elites were important in mobilizing consent and legitimacy, and in the formation of party systems. This approach has been especially usefully developed by Tarrow (1977), in the context of a comparison of France and Italy.

This brief outline of possible theoretical approaches to explaining differences in central – local relations does not suggest which of the theories is likely to prove most useful. It does show that a variety of theoretical perspectives has direct relevance to explaining different dimensions of central – local relations. Whether it is desirable or possible to fuse such perspectives into a more general theory is something that cannot be discussed here.

Yet this book remains the first stage of an enterprise in which comparative explanation is to be attempted; the concluding chapter points the way towards further comparative explanation. To explain requires something that is in need of explanation. In the conclusion, we seek to point out how the valuable descriptive detail in this book may be set out to form a clear and manageable set of differences between countries that needs explanation. The dimensions of functions, access and discretion point us in the direction of a number of relevant facts on which an evaluation of patterns of central – local relations can be based. The concluding chapter sets out a variety of criteria on which such an evaluation may be made. This evaluation, as well as an attempt to explain different patterns of central – local relations, will form the subject of a later study already in preparation.

2
Sweden

Tage Magnusson and Jan-Erik Lane

Introduction

As in the other Scandinavian countries in this study, local government in Sweden can trace its modern origins to the middle of the nineteenth century. A royal decree of 1862 sought to bring order to the rather heterogeneous structure that had prevailed for centuries, despite the constitutional reforms of 1809 and 1810 (Herlitz, 1928). The 1862 law added the county level of government (*Landsting*) and the primary local level (*Kommun*) to the existing parish councils (*Kyrkoförsamlingen*). Moreover, among the primary local government units it distinguished between the city (*Stad*), the small town (*Köping*) and the rural district (*Landskommun*). This system lasted, with minor changes until the immediate postwar period.

The 1862 reforms also guaranteed local government extensive autonomy: municipalities were given a general authority to deliver services within their area, as well as a system of taxation to finance them. However, local government expenditure and manpower levels remained low for eighty years after the reforms of the nineteenth century. Spending remained at 5–6 per cent of the Gross National Product (GNP) until the interwar years, when education, social welfare and unemployment legislation brought the proportion up to 10 per cent.

During the Second World War, a royal commission appointed to review local government pointed out the inadequacies of the system that resulted from the small size of many of its units. In 1952, the number of rural districts was reduced from 2400 to 1037. A second wave of amalgamations followed the report of a second commission appointed in 1959. This recommended a minimum population of 8000 and led to the amalgamations of 1969–74 — a process that created substantial organizations with large budgets (Gustafsson, G., 1980).

During this period, the distinction between the different types of district was abolished, so the contemporary system comprises twenty-three county councils, mainly responsible for health care, 284 municipalities, responsible for a wide variety of services, and 2286 church councils, mainly carrying out administrative functions for the parishes.

Sweden's 1975 constitution recognized the position of local government by stating that popular government should be realized through a representative and parliamentary system, and through local government.

The country is divided into municipalities (Kommuner) and county councils (Landsting). The executive power of the local governments is exercised by elected assemblies. The local governments may tax their citizens to carry out their tasks. (Chapter 1, paragraph 7).

These units are by no means the only public institutions at the local or regional level; there are numerous state organizations at both levels, but they are set apart because they are elected by the population of a distinct territory. Although all local governments carry out special functions, their distinctive feature is their autonomy within such a territory.

The postwar period thus witnessed a radical transformation of the local government system. A massive expansion of services delivered, as well as the reorganization of its boundaries and internal procedures, has served to bureaucratize local government. Moreover, this increasing bureaucratization led to increased discretion for local government within the political system, as the centre came to perceive its role less in terms of directing subservient and often unprofessional local government units, and more in terms of setting broad priorities with choice of operational means and instruments left to the local level.

Bureaucratization through expansion

Municipalities
Organizational growth has been a dominant theme in the postwar development of the public sector. The expansion of government activity has especially affected local government, which has become responsible for an increasing range of welfare services. The average yearly rise in total volume of municipal activity between 1965 and 1980 was more than 10 per cent, measured by current prices, compared with about 16 per cent between 1975 and 1980. Real economic growth averaged 6 per cent a year between 1965 and 1980, which is far in excess of the rise in GNP. Between 1970 and 1980, municipal spending increased from 13 to 16 per cent of GNP.

One important result of the amalgamation process was that the extensive citizen participation typical of Swedish municipalities was diminished; instead, formal organizations staffed by professionals and administrators were built up, as Gustafsson has shown (Gustafsson, 1980). Among policy makers and planners, it was believed that local government amalgamation would promote efficiency. More specifically, the national government and proponents of enforced, as opposed to voluntary, local government amalgamations argued that the amalgamations would help to reduce overall costs, as well as to enhance administrative efficiency — a belief that Sharpe terms the 'functional hypothesis' (Sharpe, 1978). It has been claimed that the functional hypothesis proved correct and that overall costs were less in amalgamated municipalities than they were in non-amalgamated ones. This conclusion may be called into question, because supporters of the functional hypothesis fail to take account of the differences that obtained, before, as well as after, the amalgamation.

The evidence indicates that, for the most part, the cost differential between amalgamated and non-amalgamated municipalities existed before the amalgamation. It may be shown that amalgamation did not lead to a relative decrease in costs for municipal services, except in terms of administrative charges. Instead, the amalgamation process furthered the introduction of big government to the local government system (Lane and Magnusson, 1982).

Counties
In 1960, county council spending accounted for around 2 per cent of GNP. By 1981, this had risen to 7 per cent, although GNP itself doubled over the period. Between 1972 and 1981, total county council spending rose by 336 per cent, at current prices; when inflation is taken into account, this represented an 83 per cent rise. One outcome of this period of rapid expansion was that the county councils became the sole provider of health services. Former state functions, such as responsibility for mental health, district general practitioners and the training of nurses in secondary schools, have been transferred to the county councils. But they have also entered other fields of activity including education, culture and development work. Around 75 per cent of the budget still goes to healthcare.

With the expansion of the county councils came responsibility for the planning of all healthcare activity at a county level. The councils now have a large number of planners. Moreover, they have the right to elect representatives to the state county administrative board, in order to increase co-ordination between the state regional organization and the local government system.

The local government system grew rapidly during the 1970s, as both county councils and municipalities expanded at a higher rate than annual GNP growth. Not until the early 1980s was there a reaction to local government expansion, thanks to a sharp rise in the national government's budgetary deficit. As a result of the growth of the 1970s, the municipalities and county councils were transformed into large administrative units employing a substantial portion of the workforce, and having a monopoly on the supply of various goods and services. The overall expansion between 1970 and 1980 was attended by an increase in administrative costs for both municipalities and county councils (Lane, Magnusson and Westlund, 1982).

Whether or not administrative costs include the cost of running political assemblies and the political executive, as well as the administrative costs of the various departments, spending on administration has expanded more rapidly than the municipalities' overall activity. This may be referred to as a process of bureaucratization. A similar change has overtaken the county councils. As a result of the bureaucratization process, the municipalities lost one of their distinctive features — government by lay politicians — and were transformed into bureaucratic machines, rule-bound and displaying considerable inertia in decision making. The expansion of the administration signifies a trend towards structural change in the powers of politicians, professionals and administrators — bureaucratization — that has accompanied organizational growth.

Functions of local government
The importance of local government in the Swedish political system derives in part from the fact that the municipalities are regarded as important vehicles for democracy, mobilizing citizen participation in local territorial units. In part, the importance of local government derives from its responsibility for the delivery of several important goods and services provided by the welfare state. Local government is supposed to encourage both local citizen participation and efficiency in large-scale public resource allocation, although these two goals may conflict. The first may lead to variation in the level and quality of services, whereas the second may result in standardization.

In terms of what it provides, local government is of fundamental importance to the public sector, spending as it does a large proportion of public money. Its power to raise taxes independently enables the local government system to mobilize about one-third of the public income, but it accounts for almost one-half of public expenditure. Most local government resources are taken up by the direct provision of services, as transfer payments are made either by the state or through the social insurance system. In practice, local government is more important than the state when it comes to public resource allocation. Most welfare services, including housing, health, education and social care, are provided by local government; in addition, the municipalities are active with regard to services such as roads, water supply, sewerage and garbage disposal.

Local government has a monopoly on supplies of some goods and services. Departments providing these services are important not only because of their allocation functions but because of their role as employer (see Table 1).

Between 1972 and 1982, the public sector's share of total employment rose from 32 per cent to 41 per cent; at the same time, local government's share of total public employment rose from 65 per cent to 73 per cent. The trend that began in the 1960s still holds, meaning that

TABLE 1
Sweden: public employment, 1972 and 1982
('000)

Year	Workforce total	Public employment				
		Total	State	% of total	Local government	% of total
1972	3493	1117	392	35	725	65
1982	3876	1580	431	27	1149	73

Source: Central Bureau of Statistics, *Statistisk Arbok*, Stockholm, 1977, 1982.

more and more public services are provided through the local government system. In spending terms, the municipalities are twice as large as the county councils, today disposing of about 50 per cent of total public expenditure.

The aggregate figures on spending and manpower reflect the fact that the development of the Swedish local government system is the outcome of a conscious choice of local government to be the vehicle for public-sector expansion. The present position is the result of both linear expansion and structural change. The growth of the county councils is an example of the former, whereas the development of the municipalities comprises a considerable structural change initiated in terms of a major local government reorganization.

TABLE 2
Sweden: municipal expenditure and employment, 1981

Department	Expenditure (SKr million)	% of total spending	Employees (% of total)
Education	32,223	22	37
Social welfare	27,347	19	35
Energy, fresh water	20,182	14	3
Sewerage, garbage disposal			
Land development, housing	10,818	7	2
General administration	9047	6	7
Leisure activities, culture	8895	6	4
Healthcare, environmental protection	8069	5	0.3
Transport	7843	5	2
Work, industry, commerce	5740	4	1
Other	16,807	12	7
Total	146,971	100	100

Source: Central Bureau of Statistics, Municipal Accounts, Stockholm, 1982; and Association of Swedish Municipalities, *Municipal Personnel*, Stockholm, 1982.

Let us take a closer look at the scope of local government service provision, beginning with the municipalities. Of the nine main programmes in the municipal budget, education and social welfare together constitute more than 40 per cent of the expenditure and more than 60 per cent of the workforce (see Table 2). These are the most closely regulated programmes, thanks to the School Act and the Social Welfare Act, which place responsibility for primary and secondary education, and social welfare, with the municipalities. Instructions from state agencies are very detailed in these sectors. Other programmes that are specially regulated are environmental protection, public health and housing. It is estimated that more than two-thirds of municipal budgets are generally reserved for mandatory services, although the variation between municipalities of differing size, in different parts of the country, is considerable. The mandatory share of the budget is usually larger in small municipalities, compared with big, densely populated ones. However, it is difficult to account for the variation between the municipalities because expenditure and workforce figures are not easily interpreted in service output terms. If, in 1983, mandatory services took two-thirds of the budget, the median municipality still spent about SKr4000 (roughly £400) a citizen on non-mandatory services. The latter include in principle anything that is for the common benefit of the locality: industrial infrastructure, public transport, tourism, sport and cultural activities. Even small municipalities have engaged in costly schemes to provide power stations, swimming pools, sports arenas and theatres. This is partly because several expanded their services immediately prior to amalgamation, in order to pass on the costs to the newly enlarged municipality.

The division of function between municipal and county councils is decided by law as far as mandatory services are concerned. For non-mandatory services, the replacement of the Municipal Act of 1953 and the County Council Act of 1954 by the Local Government Act of 1977 meant that the responsibilities of the county councils increased. In the 1954 Act, councils were restricted to the areas of health and hospital care, education, social care, and the development of agriculture and other forms of industry. The widening of the councils' statutory responsibilities puts them on an equal footing with the municipalities as far as the development of new services is concerned; it was argued that the division of some functions could best be decided by the county councils and the municipalities themselves. The county councils' longstanding mandatory services and the sharp rise of costs in these sectors appear to have effectively limited any ambitions they might have to engage in the provision of new types of services.

In 1981, roughly 75 per cent of the county council budget went to health and hospital care; together with other mandatory items, the

TABLE 3

Sweden: county council expenditure and employment programmes 1981

Programme	Expenditure (SKr million)	% of total	Employees (% of total)
General administration	2163	4	1
Healthcare	41,418	76	86
Social activities	652	1	1
Care of mentally handicapped	4162	8	8
Education, culture	2621	5	2
Other	3023	6	1
Total	54,050	100	100

Source: Computed from Central Bureau of Statistics, *County Council Accounts*, Stockholm, 1982; and Association of Swedish County Councils, *County Council Personnel*, Stockholm, 1982.

compulsory share bordered on 90 per cent. In the past ten to twenty years, support for industrial development has become an important responsibility for the county councils. The councils have been willing to take on more activities in this area in co-operation with the county administrative boards. However, the central government is reluctant to accept this on the grounds that it may cause problems of co-ordination with respect to centrally defined regional development policy. The county councils have expanded into fresh fields of activity, but many of their non-mandatory services take the form of additional healthcare provisions, such as maternity clinics and other specialist health centres.

Programme variation, in terms of per capita cost is substantial among both municipalities and county councils. How do we account for the cost differentials? Replicating international research, attempts have been made to estimate the impact of factors such as resources, needs and politics, but the results are not altogether satisfactory. Large-scale statistical analyses of cost variation have failed to provide a definitive answer to the basic problem of local government policy analysis, namely, the impact of various environmental determinants, including the role of politics (Murray, 1980; Johansson, 1982; Johansson, 1976). Demographic factors are relevant to the explanation of cost variation in some programmes, but what matters more are the choices of programme structure concerning size of operation, access to services and quality of service. It appears that the dimensioning of programmes is one basic explanatory factor, but how do we account for the different ways in which choices are made about programme structures? Micro-analyses of programmes indicate that there is an efficiency problem in Swedish local government service provision —

that is, some municipalities and county councils provide excessive services in terms of both quality and quantity. It is impossible to account for the policy variation by means of environmental factors, so it is apparent that the structuring of various functions has to do with choices about service quality and service quantity.

Discretion

The autonomous status of Sweden's municipalities and county councils is guaranteed by the constitution. This means that local government powers are not simply delegated from national government. In theory, the municipalities and county councils constitute the local government system because they are autonomous: all other regional and local public bodies have powers delegated from the centre. In practice, this is misleading, because local government carries out a number of functions as a result of central directives. In addition, the authorities receive a substantial portion of their financial resources from the centre. They have to reconcile their theoretical autonomy with the need to comply with a huge number of central directives about what they should do, as well as about how they are expected to do it. Not only do local authorities interact with the national government, they have also to define their relations to state organizations at the regional and local level, chief of which is the county administrative board. These state county administrative boards could be described as semi-prefectoral organizations subordinate only to the national government, charged with supervising and co-ordinating public undertakings in their region. However, the regional board's power is limited with respect to the municipalities and county councils, because of the status bestowed on them by public election, as well as by the constitution. Thus, local discretion is the outcome of an interaction between various bodies. The powers of councils and executives are to a large extent reduced by their inability to interfere in areas falling under the jurisdiction of state agencies, which are regulated by law or regulation. Although the councils may decide their own budgets, central laws or regulations often set minimum standards of service.

Local government provides services in a variety of fields. The Local Government Act of 1977 sets out the presumed form of general competence:

> Municipalities and county councils may take care of and decide upon matters of their own concern.... There are special provisions regulating the performance of certain tasks and the division of these tasks between the municipalities and county councils. (Chapter 1, paragraph 4)

The first sentence defines the so-called free field of activity and the statement '. . . matters of the their own concern. . .' gives an impression of omnicompetence. General local government competence is restricted by a set of rules interpreted by the state administrative courts. In a substantial number of rulings, these courts have laid down how the concept of local government competence is to be defined. Four fundamental norms restrict the discretion of local governments:

- *the principle of locality:* there must exist a clear connection between the activities of the local government and the interests of the population it serves
- *the principle of equal treatment:* each citizen must be treated in a similar way
- *the principle of non-profit:* local government is not allowed to charge a price higher than it costs to provide a service or goods
- *the principle of non-speculation:* local government is not entitled to engage in activity that typically belongs to the private sector, including the operation of companies and businesses.

These principles have been specified in detail in the 'kommunal-besvär', in which citizens appeal against local government decisions to a state administrative court. It should be pointed out that the courts' interpretations of the rules are occasionally rather strict, but at other times leave local government with rather more discretion. In addition, a statement in the local government Acts of 1953 and 1954 declared that local government could not engage in activities which by law should be carried out by other organizations. It was not considered necessary to incorporate it in the 1977 Act, but the provision is still in force. It is, for example, agreed that labour market and regional economic policies are matters of central government concern, but the municipalities have, nevertheless, become more and more closely engaged in various support programmes for local enterprise (Leijon, Lundin and Persson, 1984). It has been argued that, besides stretching the concept of general local government competence, this represents a clear violation of the principle of non-speculation; however, citizen appeals are rare at times of rising unemployment.

Local government has to carry out some activities in compliance with special regulations. These regulations are either in the form of laws passed by the *Riksdag* (parliament), or of detailed instructions worked out by the state agencies responsible for various areas of the public domain. Directives are sometimes tied to grant allocations.

The financial system is one of two sources of central government influence on local government policy making. The municipalities have four main sources of revenue: local income tax (42 per cent), special state grants (21 per cent), general state grant (4 per cent), charges (18 per cent) and other sources (15 per cent). The ratio between different types of revenue has been fairly stable for the past twenty years. There are no formal restrictions on local income tax, except that it is to be a proportional tax. However, central government has not refrained from attempts to influence local decision making in fiscal matters. At times of impending crisis in state finance, the centre has negotiated agreements with the local authorities to put a ceiling on tax increases. As a result, the latter tend to rely more on charges as a financial resource, although in general they have not fully explored the possibilities. In some services, tax revenues are used to cover production costs that could be paid for entirely by charges. Raising the charges would therefore cut expenditure — and strengthen the overall financial position. Because of the heavy overall tax burden, it is no longer possible for local government to raise taxes and charges without interacting with other public-sector organizations. More and more, voluntary co-ordination over revenues is seen between local and central government. At times, the latter has raised the general state grant in return for a promise on the part of local governments not to raise taxes. However, on other occasions the central government has stated that it intends to reduce the special state grants substantially. The local government system is rapidly moving towards a steady state because of an increasing strain on its capacity to raise funds, as well as the fierce competition for resources between different levels of government.

The general state grant differs from the various special state grants not only in the sense that it is much smaller in terms of money; the two programmes also have different purposes. The general state grant is supposed to even out differences in the taxation base between municipalities, whereas special state grants aim to promote the provision of certain goods and services in education and social welfare. It is an open question as to whether the general state grant really serves its purpose, as it may be claimed that its general budgetary impact is to increase total spending (Murray, 1980); special state grants, on the other hand, appear to have a more direct effect on the services towards which they are directed. The types of services that are targets for state grant subsidization are shown in Table 4.

State grants appear to be allocated in various ways, depending on the nature of the service or goods to be provided. Programmes that are less local in character tend to have a larger share of state grant funding. A programme's local orientation may have its source in local values or knowledge. Programmes whose means–end structure is not based on these sources belong to the set of national public goods, whereas the set of local public goods is based on a policy that expresses local values or is founded on a local adaptation of technology. Some programmes, such as water supplies and sewerage, or recreation and culture, are local projects in a sense that a programme such as education is not. The dis-

TABLE 4
Sweden: special state grants to local government
(per cent of income in major services)

Municipalities		County councils	
General administration	2	General administration	3
Work, industry, commerce	21	Healthcare	1
Land development, housing	21	Social activities	4
Transport	10	Care of mentally handicapped	9
Leisure activities, culture	1	Education, culture	23
Energy, fresh water, sewerage, garbage disposal	0.1		
Education	62		
Social welfare	25		
Healthcare, environmental protection	9		

Source: Computed from Central Bureau of Statistics, *Municipal and County Council Accounts*, Stockholm, 1982.

tinction here refers to whether an activity is deemed to reflect a particular local need to be based on an intimate knowledge of the local vicinity, or if it is held to reflect common national standards. In Sweden, the allocation of state grants to local government may be interpreted as a differential valuation of local variety. Whereas local values and knowledge are de-emphasized in the areas of education and social care, it is a different matter with programmes such as leisure activities. The proportion of national and local goods in local government activities reflects the strong emphasis on their welfare state role.

It has already been pointed out that different policy areas are subject to different degrees and types of central regulation. Local government autonomy or discretion may be considered as a function of the application of two distinctions: general local government competence versus competence derived from special law, and regulation versus no regulation. Thus we can distinguish four types of services delivered as part of the general competence, those with low regulation (type 1); those with high regulation (type 2); those that are mandatory, but with low regulation (type 3), and mandatory services with high regulation (type 4).

It could be argued that the 'natural' types of interaction patterns between national and local government are types 1 and 4, where non-mandatory activities go with little regulation and mandatory activities are accompanied by much regulation. The central government would be most interested in regulation when it has made activities obligatory, while regulation would be of little interest to the centre when it comes to activities undertaken by the local governments within their general competence to act autonomously. However, this is not the case. As a matter of fact, types 2 and 3 are just as likely to occur in the Swedish local government system. We have already seen that, in some areas, the interpretation of general competence by the administrative courts has resulted in a legal system that places real restrictions on local government discretion.

Perhaps the most conspicuous example of the combination of special legal competence and little regulation is to be found in local government decision making about land use and development. Central government has entrusted the municipalities with overall responsibility for the planning of land and land development — the so-called land planning monopoly. All kinds of land use and construction must be approved by the municipalities. This obligatory function has been combined with a high degree of discretion as to the kinds of activity in which the municipalities may engage in order to plan land use and construction. The municipalities' discretionary powers have been enlarged by laws allowing them to buy land they wish to develop themselves, to expropriate such land where necessary, and to negotiate contracts with private enterprise for its development. State laws not only control local government activity; they may expand its discretionary role, even within mandatory areas.

The regulated sector has had some impact on the structure of municipal organization, demanding the establishment of boards for building, healthcare, education and social welfare, as well as an election committee. Laws regulating the mandatory services provided by the county councils do not require the establishment of special boards, a factor that has led to greater variety of organizational structure than among the municipalities.

The centre controls local governments by means of two basic techniques: budgetary instruments and legal measures. Local government discretion is a function of how its internal decision making relates to external directives; grants are not unambiguous tools of control, binding only the recipient. However, it is not easy to make a general statement about the degree of local discretion in Sweden. Institutional autonomy varies with functions: some functions — the free sector — are characterized by a high degree of discretion, while others are closely regulated. Clearly many fall between the two extremes. Central government regulates the local government system by means of rules, directives and grants. Specific problems are tackled through each of these control mechanisms, meaning there is enough fuzziness in the implementation of central government plans to leave local governments with a high degree of discretion. In addition, the latter may take action on their own in several fields and they also have strong revenue powers. The expansion of the local government system has been accompanied by extensive state governance, but in a broader perspective it is apparent that the system has been strengthened, thanks to the expansion of its responsibilities.

The demand for decentralization has grown stronger during the past ten years, and the sheer weight of the local government system, combined with the development of a new administrative ideology, has resulted in the adoption of further measures to decentralize many fields. The county councils' mandatory activities used to be governed by a set of detailed rules laid down by the Riksdag and implemented by a powerful state agency, the Board of Health and Social Affairs. Vital elements of the councils' expansion plans, such as investments and the allocation of doctors, were controlled by the need for approval by the centre. There was also a system for supervising the councils' work, including a board handling malpractice complaints. In 1982, it was decided to change the relationship between the centre and the county councils to a model based on decentralization. According to the new administrative ideology, the centre is to identify the main objectives, leaving the councils with ample discretion to choose the means of pursuing them. Thus, a number of control instruments were abandoned and the position of the central agency altered to that of a general planning board.

Starting about ten to fifteen years ago, a similar development has been taking place with regard to the municipalities. The government and its agencies have become less interested in detailed issues concerning mandatory activities. Instead, the emphasis is on general planning, leaving implementation to the municipalities. This process of decentralization is a piecemeal one, proceeding at different speeds for different activities. The reorientation of administrative ideology has benefited the local government system. It is argued among centrally placed planners and decision makers that a system of detailed regulation is not conducive to efficiency in operative functions. In terms of overall goals, the demand for comprehensive planning, leaving crucial choices of means and instruments to the implementation bodies, has enhanced local government discretion. Following the trend towards introducing framework laws, the scope for institutional autonomy is definitely expanding in the Swedish local government system.

Access
The formal system of central government control over local government activity is extensive. It encompasses law, regulations and instructions regarding service production, and the organizational structure, as well as a variety of financial measures. There are also mechanisms through which local government can express its views on

national policy making. Since there has been such an emphasis on promoting equality among the local authorities, by means of national regulation, it is little wonder that local governments have sought to compensate for their lack of discretionary powers through formal and informal means of influence at the centre. Various mechanisms may be identified, including local government associations, and the use of petitions and personal contacts, as well as the party political channel.

Many members of parliament — around 80 per cent — are former local government politicians with an understanding of the problems such governments face. This may help to explain the rapid expansion in special state grants, following new regulations and instructions. It is a convention that the state reimburses local governments when they are entrusted with new functions. At times, these state grants have, in volume, exceeded by far the rate of expansion in local government responsibility, this is particularly true for the municipalities.

All municipalities are voluntary members of the Association of Swedish Municipalities (Svenska Kommunförbundet); the county councils are members of the Association of Swedish County Councils (Svenska Landstingförbundet). These organizations have come to represent their members at the national level. This means, above all, that they nominate advisers to government committees dealing with local government matters. Proposals are always referred to the associations for approval. The associations are deeply involved in national policy making, in particular with regard to local government interests. They also initiate research in different sectors of local government activity, and have an important representative role for local government opinion. The organizational structure of the municipal association is based on regional institutions; as a result, co-operative bodies have evolved within it that aim to express more forcefully the views of the municipalities in some parts of the country.

The municipalities and county councils are part-owners of various companies, either directly or through their national associations. Companies that offer consultancy services to local government on such matters as environmental protection, water and sewerage systems, and building plans, have become experts on planning and costing public services; they are often called on to make analyses and do preparatory studies for government committees. There are also a number of associations safeguarding special interests, such as the Association of Power Supply Plants and the Association of Water and Sewage Works. Local government affiliation to these associations is usually handled by the various service departments. Besides promoting efficiency in their fields, the associations often take part in public debate.

The growing number of civil servants employed by local government has often been regarded as a threat to democratic decision making, but at the same time it has been acknowledged that they do constitute a resource to their employers. Through their education and work experience, civil servants are able to meet state agency advisers on equal terms. Good connections with the administrative hierarchy can prove valuable in forming and implementing state policy. The shift to a better qualified staff in local government has had implications for the balance between centralization and decentralization. It is argued that a system of detailed state regulation restricts only the capacity of local government staff to take account of the position of their particular government, making adaptation to local circumstances possible. More and more it is argued that central government control and guidance results in excessive costs, restricting the adaptive capacity of local staff. These have a number of professional associations, for both municipal and county council employees, but membership is voluntary and they lack official recognition. Earlier, the training of many local government officials took place primarily at the colleges for social work and administration, now it is an integral part of the university system. It used to be the case that the training was mainly practical, and considered non-academic, but recent higher education reforms have attempted to upgrade the courses, including a higher academic content.

A different and more direct way to try to influence government decisions is through meetings with ministers. This is often used as a last resort, when decisions have already been made and local politicians discover that compliance will pose problems for their municipality or county. It should be mentioned that local government contacts with central government are not always channelled through the national associations. Individual authorities often visit or send petitions to the national government, pointing out special problems.

Conclusion

The role of Swedish local government has changed a great deal since the Second World War. Traditionally, it was regarded as a low-cost operation based on small territorial units run largely by amateurs; following the changes in the system during the postwar years, local government has been charged with responsibility for a major share of welfare state activities. The expansion of local government has been accompanied by the introduction of state regulations governing the provision of goods and services; state grants have changed the revenue side of the budget and a bureaucratization of local government administration is apparent. In the municipalities, the bureaucratic process was accelerated when the amalgamation reform reduced the number of elected representatives. At the same time, service activities expanded to the point where professionals were needed to administer them according to state norms. The amalgamation reform and the professionalization of local government administration were central to the policy of expanding the public sector, but they also presented a threat to popular participation at the local level. The appearance in the 1970s of activist groups and local organizations, outside the established political system, provided some indication of the frustration felt by the public, which tended to see local government as a more or less integral part of the national administrative machinery. The tension between local democratic values and national welfare state ambitions became acute and attempts at external as well as internal decentralization were made.

In 1979, the municipalities were empowered to set up neighbourhood councils and institutional boards in order to open additional channels for popular participation. Several have made use of the provisions enabling them to create new participatory mechanisms, and have run experiments with new political or functional structures. In most cases, the municipal councils have been unwilling to delegate real power to these new bodies; instead, they tend to use them as platforms for communicating decisions and presenting plans. Yet there have been examples of real delegation to institutional boards; the law on neighbourhood councils and institutional boards offers a potential means for an organizational modernization within the municipalities. Regulation of local government decision-making structures by the centre has been softened. These local bodies may have a quite different structure from the traditional decision-making mechanisms, which all have the same territorial base. The local bodies may take over responsibility in various areas — mandatory as well as non-mandatory — for a part of the local government territory. The new law thus breaks with the tradition of a unitary territorial base for decision-making bodies. It also opens up the possibility of increased local variation, because the structuring of the local organizations is to a large extent a task for the municipalities themselves. In the traditional system, central government required the municipalities to set up an assembly and various executive bodies. In addition, each mandatory activity was to be conducted under the supervision of an executive organization, which prescribed how it was to be carried out. These attempts at an internal restructuring of decision-making mechanisms within the municipalities, rather than external decentralization of state authority to local governments, reflects uncertainty about how the municipalities are to handle a changing environment. The hierarchical and fragmented decision-making system typical of the municipalities worked well in years of organizational expansion, but how are the municipalities to manage in a steady state with still-growing demands but tightening resources? It has been argued that they will have to strengthen their leadership functions when the centre allows more local discretion (Wiberg, 1985).

The central government has recently initiated a project in which eight municipalities and three county councils are to be given the freedom to restructure their administrative organizations. This autonomy is conditional in the sense that the reorganization plans must be submitted to the central government for approval. The project will be an interesting social experiment if the local authorities are given the freedom to decide how to spend their money. It may be predicted that this area of decentralization will gain further momentum in the near future. There is likely to be a trend towards greater local autonomy simply because the central government can no longer afford an expensive system of state grants — a system that, up to now, has been a principal method of regulation and control.

The sharp rise in public-sector costs has become more and more burdensome in recent years, because the revenue side has failed to keep pace. It has become clear to the state that efforts must be made to hold back local government expenditure; a politically neutral way to accomplish this is to promote efficiency and thrift. Government committees and advisory groups have repeatedly suggested that special state grants encourage excess spending. By replacing the various special grants with a large general grant, and leaving the allocation decision with the municipalities and county councils, the state hopes the money will be used more effectively. If the national government does move along this road, there must be a substantial revival in local autonomy, because the delegation of allocation decisions must be followed by a reduction in the number of regulations and instructions that are attached to all special state grants. The result will probably be greater variation in service standards among the local governments. The final decision must strike a balance between the need for public-spending cuts and an acceptance of unequal standards of service for people living in different parts of the country — efficiency and national policy demands versus local variety and decentralization.

3
Norway

Trond Fevolden and Rune Sørensen

Introduction

In some countries, such as Britain and France, it is possible to identify a high degree of continuity, stretching back at least to the beginning of the nineteenth century, in local government organization and central–local government relations in particular. In Norway, the postwar period marks a dramatic contrast with the pattern of central–local relationships that prevailed in the first part of this century. Of course, local government in Norway is an ancient institution, and the legal foundation for the modern form of local government was laid in 1837 with the passage of the Local Government Act (*formannskapslovene*). In the decades after the Act, local government activity was very limited. One indication of this is the fact that the largest item of spending in the municipality of Baerum, adjacent to Oslo, was payment of bounties to lynx hunters. The low level of local government activity is hardly surprising given the fact that the Act was pushed through the Storting (parliament) by farmers seeking to reduce public spending.

Towards the end of the nineteenth century, central government assigned three tasks to local government: care for the poor, primary education and road building. Until the end of the First World War, local authorities took on costly tasks such as building power plants and housing, and installing water supplies. Local government spending rose from around 3 per cent of gross national product (GNP) in 1890 to about 5 per cent in 1930. During the economic crisis of the 1920s, a growing burden of expenditure led a number of municipalities into bankruptcy. Consequently, the laissez faire approach to local government that had developed since the second half of the nineteenth century gave way to greater central control, with direct state supervision of bankrupt authorities (Kjellberg and Myhren, 1975). In general, state supervision expanded to such an extent that a prewar commentator noted that: 'the power that the Fylkesmand, the permanent county government and a state official, can exercise over local government is a striking feature of the system' (Harris, 1933:10–17).

Three stages of postwar development

The postwar period was one of dramatic change for Norway's local government system as the Labour Party (Arbeiderpartiet) sought to use it as a major vehicle for implementing the expansion of the welfare state. Broadly, postwar development can be broken down into three main stages marked by the shifting attitudes of central and local government to welfare state provision.

1945–63: willing central government, reluctant local government

During the early postwar period, local politicians and administrators were generally unwilling to increase the level of local government activity. There were three major reasons for this. First, a number of municipalities regarded the policies of central government as an attempt to reduce local self-rule. This impression was strengthened by the new laws instructing local government to undertake new activities. These laws imposed quite detailed rules about how such tasks should be carried out. Second, some municipalities were reluctant to increase the burden of local taxation, partly out of fear that neighbouring communes might maintain lower tax rates, thereby attracting new inhabitants. Third, the calamitous economic experiences of the prewar period led local administrators and politicians to be cautious about taking on increased financial commitments. Local authorities did not wish to risk the dangers of new economic crisis, and generally favoured private consumption rather than public spending.

To resolve some of these problems, central government in the early 1960s decided on a more comprehensive structural change, in which the reform and amalgamation of local government units were the most important elements.

Tax reforms secured relatively equal rates on taxable incomes across the country. The communes were given a new ceiling on tax rates, and all soon applied the maximum. Central authorities also strengthened the system of transfer payments, in particular the general income support grants that shifted resources from richer to poorer municipalities. Grants expanded fairly slowly until the end of the late 1960s: they stood at NKr 1920 million in 1970, an increase from the 1960 figure of NKr 953 million. During the 1970s, the growth rate accelerated quite sharply, culminating in 1980 with a grant of NKr 7595 million. (In 1983, the figure reached NKr 8192 million. All grant data computed at 1970 = 100, price index for public consumption).

Through amalgamation, the number of municipalities was reduced from about 730 in 1960 to 451 by 1970, with a slight rise to 454 in 1984 (Ostre, 1984:113). The aim of the amalgamations was to establish local units capable of implementing new public services. These required an administrative and economic base associated with a given minimum population level. Particular attention was given to the needs of primary education. In 1960, 59 per cent of municipalities had populations of less than 3000. By 1970, this proportion had been reduced to 35 per cent. Nevertheless, the Norwegian system still comprises a large number of small municipalities; by 1980, only 24 per cent contained more than 10,000 inhabitants, and nearly 5 per cent contained fewer than 1000.

1964–77: Willing central and compliant local government

The second postwar period is characterized by three important changes in the policy of central government, all giving the local authorities incentives to expand their programmes. First, instead of giving detailed instructions to local government, a revised method of drafting laws implied not only that local authorities were given new responsibilities, but also that they would enjoy a higher degree of discretion in the way they fulfilled these tasks. Second, we can observe a tendency on the part of central government to employ financial incentives to induce local government to take on new services. Central government grants made it cheaper and more attractive for local authorities to supply new services, as part of a fresh policy of inducing rather than directing them to act. Third, the legal framework and transfer system often specified which administrative and political institutions within local government were to take care of various functions. These new bodies were then responsible for their sector, giving institutionalized power to related interests and services. Such sector-based administrative bodies tended to favour expansion of local services.

In this period, the counties' administrative structure and legal responsibilities were changed fundamentally. From 1975, county councillors were elected directly. Earlier, the councils consisted of politicians — usually the mayor — elected indirectly by the municipal councils. The counties were also given powers of taxation, replacing a system of transfers from the municipalities. The establishment of the counties as an independent political unit proved to be an expansive element within the local government system. In particular, they contributed to rapidly growing expenditure by increasing capital and current healthcare spending.

1978: Willing local government, reluctant central government

Reactions at the local government level to central expansionary incentives were surprising. A number of central programmes stimulated local action, often to an extent far above expectations at the central level. Local governments undertook projects exceeding the goals of central authorities. A classic example of local performance outstripping central expectation is the introduction of a reimbursement rule of 75 per cent for current spending on local hospitals. Before this principle was established in 1970, growth in the health sector had been very modest. After its introduction the system exploded, with plans and projects clearly exceeding the goals of the central health authorities.

Central government became less enthusiastic about the expansion of local services as transfers to local government increased, as local interest groups pressed to expand local services even further, and as local employees became a large pressure group representing a significant part of the electorate.

Such a situation may be interpreted in the context of a free-rider model. At the local level, actors such as politicians, bureaucrats and special interest groups have a common interest in increasing grants from central government, in preference to raising local sources of income, such as fees and charges, or loans. As local government maximizes central transfers, leading to rapid growth in central expenditure, we can understand the political reaction of an overburdened central government. As the grant system matured and the localities became wise to its possibilities, a revision of the rules of the game became a more pressing issue.

To some extent, the system of local government financing introduced in January 1986 should change this situation. The previous system of partial reimbursements, categorical grants and general income support grants is to be replaced by one of block grants. Grants will mostly be allocated according to fixed criteria, mostly demographic and economic indicators; in this, the new system is not dissimilar from that employed in Britain.

The new revenue system has three major objectives. First, it should impose a stronger financial responsibility on local units. Second, central government provides revenues in the form of block grants, implying a lower degree of detailed financial control that may increase local discretion in the allocation of revenues. Third, the new system represents a considerable simplification, compared with the previous one of numerous smaller grants. The new regime is expected to increase the potential for rational policy making at both the central and the local level.

Figure 1 shows that expenditure, in constant 1970 terms, has grown throughout most of the postwar period. However, the period from 1949 to about 1963 is one of only modest expansion. From the mid-1960s the growth rate increases markedly, reaching its peak in the 1970s. But, towards the end of the decade, the growth in spending levels off. At this point, we enter a period characterized by an 'unwilling' central government. Figure 1 also indicates that local government consumption and investment has grown even more rapidly than total public

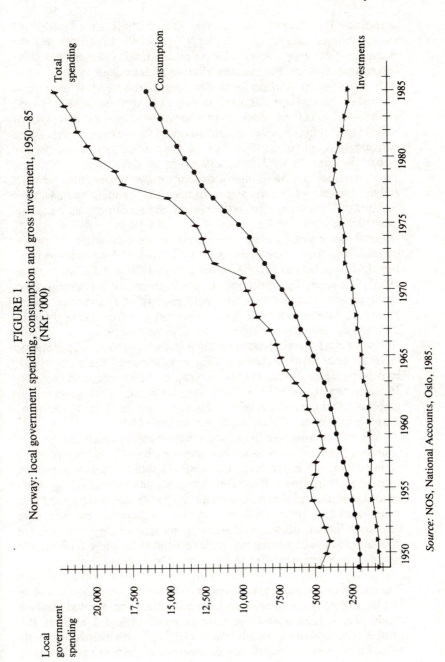

FIGURE 1

Norway: local government spending, consumption and gross investment, 1950–85 (NKr '000)

Source: NOS, National Accounts, Oslo, 1985.

spending. This means the transfers take a decreasing fraction of expenditure, a point to which we shall return. We should add that the municipalities allocate about 12.9 per cent of total expenditure to gross investment, whereas the counties allocate about 6.9 per cent.

In employment terms, local government has grown faster than central — from about 100,000 full-time equivalent employees in 1962 to about 250,000 in 1983, with the growth rate in employment following that in spending. Local and central government sectors were of roughly equal size in 1962, but the former had grown to twice the size of the latter by 1983. The postwar period has thereby produced a polity in which the communes are the main instrument for producing public services, while central government has the main responsibility for public transfers and some other national programmes, for example, defence.

Local government takes a relatively stable proportion of public expenditure: about one-third of public spending is allocated to the local level (34.1 per cent in 1960, 35.6 per cent in 1970 and 36.2 per cent in 1985). However, by restricting attention to public investments and consumption a different picture emerges. By these measures, local government has grown much faster than central — from 52.4 per cent in 1960 to 55.0 per cent in 1970, and 61.1 per cent in 1985.

Local government expenditure attained a level of about 10 per cent of GNP in 1949. This percentage held constant until the early 1960s. Expenditure has continued to rise ever since, reaching a level of about 16 per cent of GNP in 1985. In addition, local government employment, in terms of man years, has grown from about 7 per cent of the total in 1962 to almost 15 per cent in 1983.

Norway's present system of local government, in which the eighteen counties, 453 municipalities and all-purpose City of Oslo authority play an important role in providing public services, marks a strong contrast with the prewar system. The three-stage postwar development, in which central incentives played a dominant role, has to some extent produced a large structure governed by its own laws of development, which are only to a limited degree sensitive to signals emanating from central government. Let us now turn to a more detailed description of the role of local government in the contemporary Norwegian system.

The functions of local government in Norway
We have already explained how local government in Norway has two levels, the municipal and the county. Tables 1 and 2 indicate the primary functions assigned to these levels. For the municipalities, basic schooling — that is, mandatory education for children aged seven to sixteen years — takes almost one-quarter of the total budget (see Table 1). Health services are of rather less importance at the municipal level,

and mainly comprises primary healthcare, such as home nursing. More important are the social services, which take 17 per cent of total expenditure. This function comprises care for the elderly, including homes and home-help services. The municipalities also have responsibility for individuals not supported by the ordinary social security system. Religious institutions and cultural programmes constitute a mixed sector. The municipalities maintain church buildings, but do not pay stipends to the clergy. The sector also includes libraries, museums, art collections and community centres. In addition,

TABLE 1
Norway: municipal expenditure, 1979–83
(per cent of total current spending)

	1979	1980	1981	1982	1983
Central administration	5.2	5.1	5.3	5.2	5.3
Education, of which:	25.9	25.4	25.0	24.4	23.5
Basic school	22.4	21.9	21.4	20.9	20.1
Health services, of which:	10.3	11.4	11.8	11.7	13.2
Health institutions	6.9	6.8	7.0	6.8	7.0
Transfers to private and other public institution	1.5	2.6	2.6	2.6	2.5
Social insurance, etc., of which:	17.4	17.8	18.0	18.2	17.4
Social insurance	1.5	1.4	0.6	0.6	0.4
Social care	1.4	1.4	1.4	1.6	1.8
Social measures for children and youth	3.6	3.6	3.8	4.0	4.2
Care for the elderly	5.7	5.9	6.1	6.1	6.2
Home-help service	3.3	3.5	3.8	3.8	2.6
Churches, cultural programmes	3.6	4.6	5.3	5.2	5.2
Development and housing of which:	14.2	13.0	12.24	12.5	12.3
Joint admin.	2.6	3.0	2.7	3.1	3.1
Roads and streets	3.8	3.3	3.5	3.2	3.1
Water supply	1.4	1.3	1.1	1.1	1.0
Sewage disposal	0.7	0.8	1.0	1.0	1.0
Sanitary services	1.4	1.4	1.4	1.4	1.4
Fire and sweeping	1.7	1.7	1.7	1.6	1.6
Parks, baths	2.1	1.7	0.6	0.7	0.6
Housing	0.4	0.4	0.4	0.4	0.4
Development areas	0.04	0.05	0.03	0.02	0.02
Other development purposes	0.07	0.07	0.07	0.03	0.02
Municipal enterprises, of which:	17.2	16.2	16.4	16.9	16.8
Electricity plants	12.5	12.0	12.0	12.9	12.9
Other, of which:	6.0	6.0	5.9	5.9	6.3
Interest payments	4.3	4.3	4.6	4.6	4.7
Total current expenditure	100.0	100.0	100.0	100.0	100.0
(NKr, current prices)	(30,093)	(34,295)	(39,191)	45,723)	(51,680)

Source: Computed from Central Bureau of Statistics, *Statistisk Ukehefte*, Oslo, 1985.

transfers to private cultural and sports organizations are handled by the municipality's cultural administration. It should be noted that, apart from the small transfers mentioned under the social and cultural sectors, personal social services and direct running of cultural institutions are a municipal responsibility.

Municipal development and housing, encompassing water supplies, sewage disposal and other services, is another important sector. Some of these activities, for example power plants, cinemas and the management of real estate, are organized into municipal enterprises. A close look at municipal budgets reveals that this sector provides a surplus.

In 1983, the municipalities spent about NKr 516,000 million compared with NKr 317,000 million spent by the counties.

The expenditure structure of the counties is presented in Table 2. The counties are responsible for secondary education, that is, education mainly for the age group sixteen to nineteen years. These expenditures represent 16 per cent of the total. However, the major county-level function is the health services, consisting chiefly of general hospitals, psychiatric institutions and specialized medical services. Social insurance organizations, churches and cultural programmes also play a

TABLE 2
Norway: county expenditure, 1979–83
(per cent of total current spending)

	1979	1980	1981	1982	1983
Central administration	1.7	1.5	1.5	1.5	1.5
Education of which:	18.1	16.0	15.5	15.6	15.9
Secondary schools	15.8	14.0	13.8	13.5	13.8
Health services, of which:	58.7	62.7	60.2	59.5	58.7
Health institutions	44.7	39.3	38.8	38.3	37.4
Transfers to private and other public institutions	11.3	20.7	18.7	19.0	19.0
Public dentists	1.5	1.4	1.4	1.4	1.3
Social insurance	0.1	0.5	0.5	0.5	0.6
Churches, cultural programmes	0.9	0.9	0.8	0.9	0.9
Development and housing, of which:	6.5	5.4	4.8	4.5	4.4
Roads	6.3	5.2	4.6	4.4	4.2
County enterprises, of which:	10.1	9.4	9.8	10.9	11.0
Electricity plants	6.3	6.1	6.2	7.5	7.8
Harbours	2.1	1.9	2.0	1.9	1.8
Other, of which:	3.8	3.6	7.0	6.7	7.2
Interest payments	1.9	1.9	2.0	2.2	2.5
Total current expenditure	100.0	100.0	100.0	100.0	100.0
(NKr, current prices)	(15,646)	(20,254)	(24,326)	(28,115)	(31,041)

Source: Computed from Central Bureau of Statistics, *Statistisk Ukehefte*, Oslo, 1985.

minor role at the county level (see Table 2). Development and housing activity mainly encompasses roads; county enterprises consist essentially of power plants and harbours.

From a comparative perspective, it is noteworthy that neither municipalities nor counties have any responsibility for the police; this is exclusively a central government function. Nor do the communes engage much in employment and industrial policies, although some do make plans for the establishment of new business enterprises. This activity is often linked to the planning of land use within the municipalities, that is, general planning. Lastly, the municipalities produce plans for new housing. In general housing in Norway is privately owned, with public involvement largely limited to land-use planning and credit regulation.

Local government discretion
To what extent are local governments free to make political decisions within the Norwegian polity? This question may be analysed from a variety of perspectives. Taking a longitudinal approach, it may be asked whether the degree of local self-rule has been reduced or increased. A synchronic comparative perspective, in contrast, may be used to throw light on crossnational differences in local discretion. Lastly, discussions of local discretion may also be related to normative ideas regarding the proper role of local self-rule.

In addition to these perspectives, the question of discretion raises a number of methodological problems with regard to measurement and validity. We have decided to approach the question of local discretion in Norway by distinguishing four dimensions: discretion regarding the goal of communal tasks; discretion with regard to the use of local instruments; limitation of local self-rule because of central government influence on factors exogenous to local authorities; and central government influence on discretion by means of advice spread through other channels. In undertaking this analysis, we focus on the present degree of local discretion, giving attention to what we think are the distinguishing features of the Norwegian system from a comparative perspective.

The goals of local government
The basic legal foundation for local discretion is the presumption of a negatively delimited local competence; that is, local governments are free to undertake any activity not specially assigned to other public institutions. Although this definition emphasizes the discretion of local authorities, local government and local self-rule are nevertheless based on authority delegated from central government. Most laws regulating local activity assign general responsibility to the municipalities and

counties, thereby providing a fairly high degree of formal discretion.
Two important local functions represent exceptions to this rule.
First, the mandatory educational services provided at municipal and
county level are regulated in a very precise manner. The laws impose
detailed standards of service provision, such as building requirements,
the relative importance of various subjects at different class levels, the
training of teachers and so on. Second, a number of health services are
similarly regulated in substantial detail. Fifty or so laws and 150 other
regulations restrict local discretion in this field. Even so, this sector is
not centrally controlled to the same extent as education.

Local discretion in the use of instruments
Central government approves county-level decisions on important
financial matters directly through the Ministry of Labour and Local
Government, while control of the municipalities is performed by a
central government representative — the county governor (fylkes-
mannen — at the county level. As such, he or she is legally independent
of both counties and municipalities. An important function of the
county governor is that of auditing the local accounts.

Municipalities receiving income support grants (80 per cent of the
total in 1984), must send their budget to the County Governor for
formal approval. It is not unusual for budgets to be returned to the
municipalities because the estimated growth in revenues appears unreal-
istically high. In this way, central authorities can, at least to some extent,
force the municipalities to present realistically balanced budgets.

TABLE 3
Norway: municipal revenue structure, 1979–83
(per cent of total revenue)

	1979	1980	1981	1982	1983
Income tax	38.1	37.6	38.8	37.8	35.9
Transfers from central government for special purposes	11.4	14.2	14.0	14.2	14.2
Fees and charges	19.4	17.0	17.6	18.7	19.0
Income support grants	2.6	2.6	2.7	2.9	2.8
Transfers from other public sectors	2.5	3.9	4.0	4.1	4.1
Investment revenue	3.4	3.3	3.0	3.0	3.3
External loans	7.0	6.7	6.2	5.0	4.9
Funds, etc.	4.4	3.7	3.3	2.1	3.0
Others	11.2	10.4	10.4	12.2	12.8
Total	100.0	100.0	100.0	100.0	100.0
(NKr '000)	(42,723)	(46,923)	(53,374)	(60,761)	(68,573)

Source: NOS, *National Accounts*, Oslo, 1985.

The nature of the local government revenue system constitutes an important limitation on local discretion. The basic structure of local revenue is shown in Tables 3 and 4. At the municipal level, income tax represents about 35 per cent of total revenue, having declined, in relative terms, for the past ten years. These revenues are collected as a proportion of taxable personal income. The municipalities are not allowed to take more than 13.5 per cent of personal income; all currently apply the maximum rate.

About 20 per cent of municipal revenue consists of categorical grants, and 3 per cent comes from income support grants. These transfers from central government have risen quite sharply in recent years. It should be mentioned that, although the income support grant represents a modest proportion of total revenue, these transfers are especially important to small municipalities with low income tax revenue, and in some cases may provide up to 40 per cent of total income.

The residual revenue sources include surpluses from municipal enterprises, transfers from other parts of the public sector, and fees and charges.

At county level, income tax provides a smaller proportion of total revenue — less than 30 per cent. These revenues represent 7.5 per cent of taxable personal income, the highest rate allowed by central government, and currently applied by all the counties. Central government transfers, in contrast, play an even more important role at the county level, comprising about 50 per cent of total revenue. This proportion has grown substantially in recent years.

TABLE 4
Norway: county revenue structure, 1980–83
(per cent of total revenue)

	1980	1981	1982	1983
Income tax	28.0	28.0	26.9	26.7
Transfers from central to local government for special purposes	33.9	36.3	36.5	37.3
Fees and charges	10.3	10.6	11.0	11.3
Income support grant	7.5	7.6	8.1	7.5
Transfers from other public sectors	3.8	3.7	3.4	3.3
Investment revenue	1.6	1.1	1.1	1.1
External loans	4.5	4.4	3.3	3.7
Funds, etc.	2.4	1.6	1.8	1.4
Other	8.0	6.7	7.9	7.7
Total	100.0	100.0	100.0	100.0
(NKr '000)	(24,554)	(28,466)	(32,929)	(35,318)

Source: NOS, *National Accounts*, Oslo, 1985.

In general, local government is increasingly dependent on direct financial support from the centre, whereas local sources of revenue play a decreasingly important role (see Tables 3 and 4). From a cross-national perspective, it should be noted that property taxes do not provide significant revenue to the communes, and that local government has almost no discretion in setting personal income tax rates.

In order to evaluate the impact of these restrictions on local discretion, we have computed a standardized measure of variation in per capita current expenditure for various functions. This measure, the coefficient of variation (CV), is computed as the ratio of the standard deviation over the mean value. Although this is an appropriate formula for measuring dispersion, at least two factors may produce variable results. First, if the communes employ divergent accounting procedures, the CV coefficient may give an excessively optimistic picture of dispersion. Second, the per capita costs of providing a particular service level may differ substantially between communes. The CV coefficients may therefore exaggerate differences in service levels. Bearing these weaknesses in mind, the results are presented in Table 5.

The coefficients of variation for education expenditure are relatively low (0.23 in municipalities, 0.13 in counties), compared with the other sectors. Health service expenditure varies quite a lot at the municipal level, but not at the county level (0.11). Even though some of the variations within the municipal health service may be due to divergent accounting procedures, it is nevertheless surprising that the variations are so wide. Expenditure on development and housing, and municipal

TABLE 5
Norway: expenditure variation in municipalities and counties, 1974−82
(coefficients of variation for gross per capita current expenditure for
municipalities (N = 454) and counties (N = 18))

| | Municipalities | | | Counties | | |
	1974	1979	1982	1974	1979	1982
Central administration	0.30	0.38	0.49	0.32	0.36	0.26
Education	0.24	0.22	0.23	0.14	0.13	0.13
Health services	1.54	1.49	1.21	0.20	0.15	0.11
Social insurance, etc.	0.28	0.45	0.47	0.73	0.75	0.56
Churches, cultural programmes	0.35	0.41	0.42	0.52	0.22	0.28
Development and housing	0.47	0.40	0.38	0.24	0.30	0.31
Municipal enterprises	1.13	1.99	1.44	1.60	1.45	1.31
Other	0.46	0.47	0.54	0.34	0.43	0.58
Total	0.18	0.28	0.26	0.25	0.21	0.22

Source: Norwegian Social Science Data Services, *Kommunedatabasen*; Central Bureau of Statistics, *Strukturtall for kommunenes økonomi*, Oslo.

enterprises, appears to vary quite sharply between municipalities and between counties.

From a crossnational perspective, it is important to remember that per capita expenditure may be a poor indicator of service level. The variations in spending can be explained partly by cost differences between the communes resulting from, for example, varying geographic conditions and demographic structures. Furthermore, it is likely that the considerable differences in area between municipalities and counties leads to wide expenditure variations because of economies and diseconomies of scale. Counties with a more even population distribution among communes may have smaller CV coefficients, but wider variations in service level.

Local adjustment to exogenous events
So far, we have discussed ways in which central government directly influences local discretion. However, some central government policies have important indirect implications for communal discretion. Two areas are of interest here.

First, central government policy towards local authorities as employers has significant effects because of the labour- intensive nature of local service provision. For example, the introduction of worker protection legislation specifying maximum working hours led to substantial cost increases at the local level. Another example is the system of wage negotiations. These are usually completed in the private and central government sectors before discussions are started at the local level. Settlements at these other levels are often used as a model for those in the local sector, implying that the state of municipal finance has a very modest impact on the settlements reached.

Second, central government influences local discretion by its general credit policy. By regulation through private and public banks, and through its influence on interest rates, the centre may increase or decrease financial pressures on local budgets. Central government has also issued rules restricting the use of credit for financing local government activity.

Central government advice to the communes
In much the same way as in other countries, advice from the centre to local government in Norway is distributed through various channels. These include circulars, informal contacts between sector administrators at local and central levels, and the massive flow of information from government ministries. This advice may limit discretion to the extent that central government influences local preferences or local perceptions — ways of thinking — in general. Although it is extremely difficult to evaluate the impact of these

intangible channels of influence, it appears that the central authorities have used them to some extent to homogenize the preferences and perceptions of local government.

On the other hand, the establishment of local professional bureaucracies and expertise has probably increased communal autonomy. Local government has become less dependent on central advice and more capable of solving its problems without recourse to the centre. The growth of local bureaucracies not only contributes to local autonomy; it may be argued that the increasing professionalization of local administration has made it easier for the centre to implement ambitious reforms according to national standards. We suggest that the new lines of communication between professional administrators at local and central levels have broadened the potential for influence from the centre. Whether this development has led to reduced local influence is an open question. We shall return to this subject in the next section.

Local government access
The system described so far is one of mutual dependence between central and local government. Local authorities have general competence and deliver a number of services of basic importance for citizens' welfare. On the other hand, municipal revenues are constrained by central government. Therefore central government to a large extent controls the service level of its local counterparts, and is held responsible for the state of these services and for the state of local finance in general. The situation seems to open up decision-making processes at the centre to local influence.

Local access to the centre is particularly visible in those areas where central policies are dependent on information from the communes. In an effort to influence centrally made decisions, this information may be coloured or even distorted. Local governments wishing to maximize their transfers may present their position as critical, thereby exerting pressure on the central authorities to increase transfers to the particular county or municipality.

In an earlier analysis, we showed how some municipalities are able to raise spending above their revenues, thereby producing budget deficits and ultimately financial crisis (Fevolden and Sorensen, 1983). The threat of subsequent cutbacks in services then becomes a strategy for securing increased aid, in particular in the form of income support grants. In short, we may say that local governments have access to and may influence central decision making if the central authorities perceive their position to be financially depressed.

However, to the extent that the strategic situation creates an incentive to overspend, there is good reason to believe that the outcome is far from optimal. One may also doubt the equalizing effect of income support grants if this kind of 'strategic' behaviour varies from one local authority to another. The new revenue system, based on block grants distributed mainly according to fixed criteria, may reduce the incidence of this strategic behaviour.

At the national level, one may ask whether central government targets for the growth of local spending have been met. A comparison of the goals presented in the national budget (that is, ex ante) with the data presented in the national accounts (that is, ex post) provides a rough indication of the degree of central control of the economy. From 1972 to 1984, the average planned growth in local expenditure was 3.3 per cent, but the real figure averaged 5.6 per cent (Bruknapp and Sand, 1985). Although the targets may to some extent be of a normative rather than a predictive nature, these data indicate a somewhat limited central control over local spending.

Lastly, a preliminary study indicates that, in years in which local elections are held, growth in central government grants and communal expenditure has been higher than in other years. Time-series analysis of the period from 1949 to 1983 indicates that in local election years, central government transfers grew by an additional 0.6 per cent, compared with other years, local investment by 2.5 per cent, and local consumption by 1.1 per cent. However, the growth rate varies quite substantially from one period to another. This may be interpreted as one result of local access to central decision making — local politicians maximizing their election prospects by providing better services.

The institutional structure of Norway's political parties may be of some interest in this respect. First, the nomination of parliamentary candidates takes place at municipal and county levels; the central party organization has very little influence on who is given a relatively 'secure' position on the election list. As each member of parliament (MP) represents one county, the representatives have at least some incentive to act as spokesmen for local government at the national level. Second, local councils provide the major platform for recruitment to the Storting (parliament). About 85 per cent of MPs in 1985 were former member of local councils. There are good reasons to believe that members of the Storting are aware of local issues and are sympathetic to the concerns of the local authorities in their constituencies, and thus represent local interests at the national level.

It is important not to exaggerate the impact of these institutional features, however. Party differences within parliament are more important than geographical controversies. The recruitment of representatives may well produce a reservoir of understanding and support for local government in parliament. Whether or not this means that local government can exert effective influence on parliamentary decisions is an open question.

In this respect, we should mention the communes' interest organization, the Norwegian Association of Local Authorities (Norske Kommuners Sentralforbund (NKS), to which all municipalities and counties belong. The NKS attempts to influence central government decisions, and is represented on various committees dealing with local government. It also exercises influence by negotiating wage settlements with local labour unions.

However, the NKS has no regular or formal contact with central government agencies. Its influence depends on invitations to comment on central government policy proposals, giving it rather limited access to the central decision-making process.

Conclusions
In forty years, local government in Norway has developed from a relatively subordinate institution, with direct responsibility for few major tasks, to one with substantial discretion in providing many of the basic public services. The transformation of the local government system reflected, as was shown in its three-stage development, changing political attitudes and relationships throughout the period. However, the process of change was also embedded in a set of more enduring cultural values, which served to shape the policy outcomes of the changing configurations of political attitudes and relationships. Above all, the resulting pattern of functional allocation, discretion and access reflected the importance attached to local identity, geographical equity and macroeconomic governance in the Norwegian system. By exploring these values, and how they affected the postwar development of the local government system, we may not only help to explain the development of local government in Norway, but also throw light on why other polities, in which these values may have received less emphasis, developed different patterns of central–local relations.

With regard to local identity, it should be remembered that Norway is a large country with a population spread out in communities that historically have been separated by high mountains or poor communications. This has produced strong local commitments and feelings of belonging to a particular community. The impact of local identity can be seen in the persistence of relatively large numbers of municipalities. These municipalities express, at least at a symbolic level, the value of self-determination. In terms of functions, this may produce a local government system with a negatively delimited competence, and a wide range of functions with a high degree of discretion. With respect to access, the value of local identity has resulted in local councils and municipal party organizations becoming the dominant source of recruitment to national politics.

The concept of geographical equity refers to the view that living standards should not differ too much between counties and between municipalities; public services should be fairly evenly distributed across the country. It should be remembered that the relatively large number of municipalities itself acts to increase variations between the communes. These variations are all the more significant, from the perspective of central government, because of the extensive functions of local government. In order to achieve functional equality, a complex system of revenue support grants and function-specific reimbursements has been introduced. In this respect, of course, discretion has been reduced by the creation of numerous central standards to which local services must be adjusted. In addition, the fairly large number of communes has reduced the potential for direct access to central decision-making bodies. As a result, access is relatively formal.

The concept of macroeconomic governance refers to the prominent position of macroeconomic planning in Norwegian politics, partly because of the strong priority given to reducing unemployment (an aim formally incorporated into the constitution, in contrast to local self-rule), and partly because the planning agencies are centrally placed in the decision-making apparatus (within the treasury), giving them direct political access. Local functions are therefore restricted to those of minor macroeconomic significance, mostly public services to individuals, although these services may themselves be very costly. In addition, local discretion has been curtailed by a high degree of central control over local revenues. Both municipalities and counties have, at least in the short term, fixed rates of income tax. The imposition of balanced budgets and central regulation of the use of credit financing produces a highly revenue-constrained local government. At the same time, this creates a position of mutual interdependence between central and local actors. Local government is heavily dependent on central financing on various services, while central government is held responsible, in political terms, for the successes and failures of communal activity. This opens up central decision-making processes to local government pressure; that is, it allows some degree of local access.

We envisage, therefore, that the concepts of local identity, geographical equity and macroeconomic control could be important dimensions in explaining the specific nature of central–local relations in Norway, as opposed to the other unitary states of West Europe. This is a point to which the editors devote some attention in the conclusion to this volume.

4
Denmark

Peter Bogason

Local government in the Danish political system

Denmark's local government in its modern form stems from the beginning of the nineteenth century. In 1803, an Act of Parliament established a system of elected poor law commissioners; the 1849 Constitution established the principle of local self-government and was followed by the 1857 Municipal Government Act, which expanded the rights of municipalities. County government was regulated by the 1867 Country Communal law. Under the system that lasted from the second half of the nineteenth century to 1970, the national territory contained three types of local government: twenty-five counties (*Amtskommuner*), eighty-eight towns (*Kobstad*) and 1257 parishes (*Sognekommuner*). The origins of the towns go back to mediaeval times. Until the mid-nineteenth century, trade and industry not directly related to agriculture was restricted to the towns, which, as a result, were natural centres for almost all economic activity. These rights were granted by the Crown, which in turn could influence the government of the towns. Until 1919, the mayors were appointed by the king. The towns took care of all local services and were subject to review by the Ministry of the Interior.

Outside the towns, local government had two tiers. The smaller was the parish, which had carried out some schooling and social assistance since the nineteenth century. Parishes varied greatly in size and population, and their many tasks were performed with the collaboration of their neighbours, where these were small, or of a nearby town. The counties which can also trace their origins back to mediaeval times, were larger entities: there were twenty-five of them in 1965. Their main functions were to run hospitals and look after major roads. The county council was chaired by a state prefect, who also headed supervision of the parishes. The council was supervised by the Ministry of the Interior.

The revenue system was complex. Counties relied on property taxes; towns and parishes on property taxes and personal income tax. In addition, there were a few minor categorical grants and numerous

*The author wishes to thank William Andersen, Marius Ibsen, Paul-Erik Mouritzen, Bent Schou, Carl-Johan Skovsgaard and Soren Villadsen, who commented on earlier drafts of this chapter.

state reimbursement schemes, as well as a system for equalizing local personal income tax.

The local government system was increasingly perceived to be unsatisfactory. Most parishes were so small that they could not solve major problems with their own resources. Furthermore, most had no professional staff, apart from a few clerks. As a result, the expansion of the public sector took place mainly through state agencies, a mix of state–local organizations, or complex procedures involving different public agencies. In particular, many parishes co-operated in building and running primary schools and homes for the elderly; small ones often relied on the nearest town for technical assistance in road maintenance, sewerage and related fields. This the Interior Ministry found to be unwarranted, first because it believed financial responsibility was undermined by intergovernment co-operation, and second because it was obvious that most of the towns were perfectly capable of administering their many tasks, while most of the parishes were not. These differences in capability created tensions among local governments. The towns pressed for more decentralization; the state was reluctant to accede because it felt such a move might increase variations in public service between town and country.

In 1958, a commission was set up by parliament to devise solutions to the problem of local government structure, and over the following twelve years the present structure was created (Harder, 1973; Bruun and Skovsgaard, 1980). Most parish mergers resulted from local bargaining — under firm advice from the secretariat of the commission, which performed a large-scale analysis of feasible mergers. Some of the larger towns had to have their structure decided by Act of Parliament, again based on the secretariat's findings.

In sum, the reform of local government produced a two-tier elected administration structure for the whole country, apart from the metropolitan area, which, like so many other big city areas, faced special problems. From 1967, local governments co-operated voluntarily to establish a regional planning authority, and in 1974 that structure was given formal status and its powers extended to public transport, hospital planning and environmental protection. Although some dissatisfaction remains — partly because the council is not directly elected — two more recent commissions were unable to recommend any changes.

Other reforms followed in the wake of the mergers. First, local government functions were reallocated in the 1970s in order clearly to identify responsibilities within the new structures. The enlarged county councils were allocated those services that the smallest of the new municipalities could manage: secondary schools and hospitals. Those left to the municipalities were primary schooling, social security and assistance, individual health, local roads and the environment. Second, a financial reform was implemented in the mid-1970s. In order to enhance a sense of financial responsibility, a number of state reimbursements and categorical grants were replaced by a block grant. The total value of the block grant, which is similar to the general revenue sharing grant in the United States, was to be kept at a level indexed to the value of the old transfers. A system of reimbursement remained for the social assistance programmes, at a fixed 50 per cent level of most running costs. Pensions, including those for the elderly, were fully reimbursed. From 1973, counties were allowed to tax personal incomes, reflecting the need for greater resources to manage the new functions.

Third, in 1977 came a budgetary and accounting reform designed to make budgets and accounts comparable, and to oblige local governments to budget for four years ahead. This made it possible to assess the total public budget and analyse it in detail.

Overall, the reforms meant that the number of local government units was reduced, especially in rural areas and around the cities; a two-tier system (county/municipal) was established, and local governments were made more responsible, in financial terms, for the services they provided. Other measures were closely associated with the general reforms; we shall deal with these in more detail below. To generalize, one could say that the reforms aimed to increase effectiveness in so far as they gave rural areas access to all types of local government services. This was not the case in the more remote areas before 1970. Furthermore, the reforms aimed to promote efficiency in local government administration — at the cost of reducing the number of smaller entities and building up larger bureaucratic structures.

In the local government system created by the reforms, the municipalities, of which there are 275, form the lowest level. They vary in population from 2700 to 500,000 inhabitants, with an average 18,500; half have a population of 5000 to 10,000. The municipalities cover the entire national territory, except a few small islands, and deliver most daily services to the population. They are supervised by a review committee composed of four members of the county council, chaired by a state administrative officer.

County councils number fourteen, and their population ranges between 47,000 and 630,000; half have between 200,000 and 300,000 inhabitants. They deliver services that are beyond the financial means of a normal municipality. The councils are supervised by the Ministry of the Interior.

County councils do not cover the City of Copenhagen and Frederiksberg, which form the capital; these two local governments also carry out the functions of a county council. In the metropolitan area, formed by the capital and the three surrounding counties, a special council — the metropolitan council — is responsible for regional planning and public transport. The council is indirectly elected; it consists of county and municipal councillors from the area. Elections to the county and municipal councils are held every four years. Most municipal councils have between fifteen and twenty-five seats; Copenhagen has fifty-five and the three largest cities up to thirty-one. Each council elects one of its members to serve as mayor.

Collectively, these local institutions are responsible for a large proportion of total government spending. Table 1 indicates levels of central and local government expenditure since 1945. These levels are related to gross factor income (GFI — pre-1970) or gross national product (GNP — 1970 and after). The percentage has been rising steadily, almost quadrupling in thirty-five years. However, the table does not reflect the true level of expenditure, because central government grants and reimbursements to local government are included in the central government figures.

If we look at actual spending, local government expenditure in 1982 accounted for 33.5 per cent of GNP; the share of central government

TABLE 1
Denmark: Public expenditure, 1945–82
(DKr million)

	Central[1]	% of GFI	Local[2]	% of GFI
1945	1705	12.2	781	5.6
1955	4272	14.9	2306	8.0
1965	14,661	21.5	6803	10.0
		% of GNP		% of GNP
1970	36,458	30.6	14,709	12.4
1975	75,928	34.9	32,208	14.8
1980	149,843	40.0	62,533	16.7
1982	209,743	44.6	76,973	16.4

Sources: Figures for 1945–65 are from Rolf Nordstrand, *De offentlige udgifters vaekst i Danmark*, memo. No. 41, University of Copenhagen (mimeo). Figures for 1970–82 are computed from *Statistisk 10-års oversigt*, various years. Percentages for GFI are somewhat higher than for GNP — in 1970 by about five percentage points (state) and two percentage points (local). The figures from the two sources are not strictly comparable.
Notes:
1. By 'central' is meant central government's own expenditure, plus unemployment insurance fund schemes.
2. By 'local' is meant county plus municipal (town and parish) expenditure, plus health insurance fund schemes for the years before 1973.

was reduced to 27.6 per cent. The importance of local government in public service production is again clearly demonstrated by employment figures. In 1984, local government in Denmark employed about 475,000 people (full-time equivalent). This represents around one-fifth of the total workforce, and about 60 per cent of total public-sector employment. State employment totalled around 200,000.

So, by any measure, Danish local government is big. It spends funds equivalent to one-third of GNP; one of five workers is employed by a local authority. As we shall see in more detail below, local government is involved in the delivery of all public services except defence, foreign affairs, law enforcement and communications.

II
The functions of local government

Table 1 showed the growth of government after the Second World War. The relation of local to central government revenue has remained fairly constant, with the former accounting for about one-third of all public income. However, local government accounts for more than one-half of all actual public expenditure, as we shall explore in more detail later.

The division of labour between counties and municipalities is based informally on the 'subsidiarity' principle. Services that are beyond the resources of a small municipality — up to 5000 inhabitants — are generally taken over by the county; these include hospitals, secondary education, major roads, and so on. This leaves the municipalities with those functions most closely related to the daily problems of the inhabitants.

Table 2 gives a breakdown of local government expenditure and personnel. The largest category is social services and primary healthcare. The counties pay for primary healthcare, providing about one-eighth of the total cost. The municipalities provide social services: cash benefits, children's day care and varied assistance to the elderly, including rest homes. They are also responsible for a variety of social security entitlement programmes, such as pensions and sickness allowances, plus assistance programmes — determined on an individual basis — for those who have no other source of income. Unemployment benefit is administered by private insurance schemes on the basis of state mandates, but 80 per cent of the cost is paid by the state because premiums do not cover the present high level of payments. The system was established when unemployment was low.

Education and culture forms the second-largest group of services. The counties provide secondary education for sixteen to nineteen year

TABLE 2
Denmark: local government expenditure budgets by sector, 1985

	Current	Capital	Personnel
Expenditure			
Housing and environment	3.2	29.5	2.5
Transport and utilities	6.6	18.5	3.5
Roads	2.2	14.3	2.3
Education and culture	13.2	7.8	20.6
Hospitals	11.8	10.7	20.0
Social services and primary			
health	56.0	14.5	39.3
Administration, etc	6.9	4.7	11.8
Total (per cent)	99.9	100.0	100.0
Total (DKr million)	198,663	9592	447,804
Income			
Charges, fees, etc.	17.0		
Income tax, etc.	36.3		
Property taxes	2.6		
Reimbursements	32.2		
Block grants, etc.	11.6		
Total percent	100.0		
Total income (DKr million)	202,235		

Source: Ministry of the Interior, *1985 Budget*, Copenhagen, November 1984.

olds aiming to take the school-leaving examination required for university entry. The state organizes vocational schools and university education. The municipalities are responsible for primary schools and local libraries, as well as most other cultural activity.

Hospitals are run by the counties; there are no private ones. Although primary healthcare is paid for mainly by the counties, the doctors work as private practitioners, based on the fee-for-service principle. The hospitals take about 80 per cent of all health costs. All hospital treatment and most other health services are provided free of charge to the patient.

Unlike the position in many other countries, housing is not a major local government function. Most apartment housing is private, but some non-profit organizations have been set up to build and run low-income housing (Danish Ministry of Housing, 1978). These account for approximately fifteen per cent of all housing in Denmark. They receive state and local government subsidies through interest concessions and advantageous repayment periods. Municipal councils normally have one or more representatives on the board of such a company, and the number of low-rent apartments is regulated by local zoning procedures.

There is no general pattern to public transport provision. Some municipalities run buses, others rely on private enterprise and the state bus companies. The counties may also be involved, often through a countywide joint venture based on private subcontractors. Local roads are built and maintained by the municipalities, county and state roads by the counties. Services such at water, sewerage and gas are often run by the municipalities.

In comparative perspective, it is worth noting that police services are run by the central government; before the Second World War, some were controlled by the towns. However, firefighting is a municipal responsibility, although it is often contracted out to the Falck Rescue Company.

What is left for the central government? Defence, foreign affairs, railways, telecommunications and industrial development. The centre used to be solely responsible for labour policy, but steadily increasing unemployment rates have produced considerable local government involvement in the provision of special jobs for the long-term unemployed and in programmes designed to reduce youth unemployment. It is no wonder that, in personnel terms, local government grew so rapidly after the reforms of the early 1970s; all over the country, there are modern administrations, often with a high proportion of professionals within them. The changes may not have been great in the larger urban areas, but in the rural areas the range of services has increased vastly.

Local government discretion

The constitutional position
Denmark's Constitution states that 'the rights of local government independently to take care of their affairs supervised by the state is to be decreed by law.' However, this has never meant that local government may engage only in activity that is permitted by law. Local government may perform activities that relate to local problems and that are not forbidden by law or by administrative (supervisory) practice. Furthermore, it must engage in activities that are specified in particular laws. And in some cases, local government must adhere to certain standards if it chooses to engage in activity that is permitted rather than mandated.

The statutory framework for local councils is regulated by Act of Parliament. This Act (No. 623, December 1980) sets rules for the membership of a council, procedures for electing mayors and committee members, regulations about *per diems* for council members and the powers of the mayor, and rules for budgets and accounts, and for supervision.

The Interior Ministry has established a model set of standing orders for the municipalities and the counties designed to prescribe the form of standing orders that each council should adopt. These must then be approved by the minister. The model standing orders allow room for adaptation to local conditions regarding matters such as number of members, types of committee, and levels of fees and compensations. The council is permitted to decide its own operating procedures within the limits specified.

Supervision of local government takes several forms. There is general supervision of the legality of decisions, including budgets and accounts. The municipalities are supervised by a board containing four members of the county council, but chaired by the centrally appointed regional state prefect (*Amtmand*) whose administration staffs the secretariat. County councils and the two capital municipalities are supervised by the Minister of the Interior. Decisions found to be illegal may be invalidated, and if local councils wilfully neglect to make decisions required by the law, the members involved may be fined.

Within most policy fields there exist more specific forms of supervision. In social affairs, there are special regional boards and a central agency for handling complaints. In education, some complaints may be taken to the county council or even to the minister. In physical planning, the Minister of the Environment may call in plans before they are adopted by the municipality, as well as handling complaints about the procedures it follows.

These are just a few examples of the ways in which higher levels of administration can become involved in local government decision making. The pattern is complex and differs among policy fields. The present system of central−local relationships was set up in a piecemeal fashion by the 1970 reforms.

These reforms were part of a broader change in the political and administrative system, which entailed the rapid expansion of administrative agencies and an increase in central government intervention in economic and social life, as the rapid increase in public expenditure shows. Parliament, too, has gradually changed its role: its acts are less detailed than before and allow ministers to specify service requirements in more detail. Many parliamentary committees have become standing committees that seek to monitor the administration of the law (Damgaard, 1977).

The change from detailed to enabling legislation increased the importance of the central government agencies, by specifying in detail how laws affecting local government were to be applied. But in so far as the central administration was often reluctant to go very far in detailing parliamentary legislation, although with wide variation among ministries, local government in principle was often allowed wide discretion to decide these matters. For example, local government's role in social affairs before 1976 was that of an executive agency of central government, administering detailed rules or subject to central approval for specific decisions. A social welfare reform of 1976 introduced a very high degree of local government discretion in the field of social assistance and personal social service, in the level and quality of childcare services and in care for the elderly. Over time, however, more administrative rules have been established by the Ministry of Social Affairs.

The central administration did not reduce its requests for information about local government activity. On the contrary, more information was gained as a result of the introduction of mandatory sectoral planning in the major policy fields (Bogason, 1980). In some cases, such plans were subject to approval by the minister, more important was the fact that the local authorities were compelled to give structured and standardized information about local activities to the central administration.

To generalize, it seems fair to say that the role of local government in many fields was changed from one of policy implementation to one of policy planning and implementation, giving new possibilities for variations in service among localities due to differing priorities and use of capabilities. The aim was to increase the influence of local politics, but this did not mean a growth of new, locally based political parties. On the contrary, the national parties have gained momentum. But other channels have been created for local participation in public-service decisions. New physical planning statutes have increased the number of points at which the public may participate in the formulation of structural plans, and the parents of pupils in nurseries, kindergartens and schools are formally represented on the management bodies of those institutions.

By and large, these changes have come about through a shift in central−local relationships involving less specification of the detailed substance of local policies and greater emphasis on mandating procedures for local decision making. Central government changed its role from one that was primarily supervisory to one that is largely advisory — working on planning manuals, or initiating and accessing research on alternative ways of providing services — but continues to keep an eye on variations among localities and attempts to influence those local governments that are thought to deviate more from the norm than national politicians or influential professionals find acceptable. Central government supervision, then, has to a large extent changed from control over the legality of decisions and/or their approval, to a review of the adequacy of local initiatives and/or bargaining over the content of plans. Of course, heated controversies can still occur over the legality of specific decisions.

Output variations
One indication of the scope for local discretion is the variation in service quality and quantity among local governments. Of course, there are many problems involved in using such an indicator. To state that, in the County of Copenhagen school expenditure per pupil is nearly 50 per cent above average, says nothing about the potentially greater need for special educational priorities in some low-income areas. Nor does it tell us anything about the political forces at work in the decision-making process that seek to discriminate in favour of certain population groups in the locality. However, a number of studies have been made to illustrate the variations, some in the wake of the general reforms of the 1970s, and some to discuss the role of politics when new tasks are introduced to local government.

Systematic geographic differences can be found among many municipalities: Table 3 shows such differences, based on a service-level index. This index is computed as the actual current spending of a municipality, divided by the 'need' of that municipality — expressed as the current spending required if that municipality had the average per capita spending pattern. The higher the index, the higher the service level in that area. The metropolitan area has higher service levels than the rest of the country. Other data indicate that, the higher the taxable income level, the less need for public services — but the higher the actual service level. The better-off municipalities spend more money per capita on services than the less wealthy do — and it

TABLE 3
Denmark: service levels by area, 1984
(Average for all = 100)

	Municipal	County
Capital[1]	116	120
Metropolitan area	117	102
Zealand and islands	94	97
East and South Jutland	95	94
West and North Jutland	89	95

Note:
1. The functions of Copenhagen and Frederiksberg are assigned as county or municipal functions, according to the pattern prevailing in the rest of the country.
Source: Dilling-Hansen et al. (1985:39).

seems that state grants are not able to equalize the cost pattern. The result is that people in less wealthy areas pay relatively more tax for relatively poorer services (Dilling-Hansen et al., 1985).

Table 3 also indicates variations in county-level services. It appears that the two capital municipalities, which also have county functions, have an extraordinarily high level of service. Variations in the rest of the country are not as great as between the municipalities.

The pattern of party political influence on local government expenditure varies among policy fields. For example, spending on roads is not affected by the party composition of the municipal council. But on a left –right scale, socialist parties have been found to have a positive influence on spending on care for the elderly and education for disadvantaged children (Bruun and Skovsgaard, 1980; Madsen, 1984). At the same time, municipalities with fewer problems within a policy field tend to spend relatively more on each client than those with many. For example, localities with comparatively few old people spend more on each, and localities that are relatively rich and have relatively few young unemployed — factors that clearly co-variate — tend to spend relatively more on youth unemployment programmes (Bruun and Skovsgaard, 1980; Cauchi, 1984). In line with this finding, municipalities with the greatest need for intervention, because they had large numbers of unemployed, spent relatively less — and had a low level of public service anyway.

Central mandates have had some influence on spending patterns: for example, they have affected expenditure on primary schools, and low-spending municipalities spent no more than the mandatory minimum on youth unemployment programmes (Cauchi, 1984; Madsen, 1984).

Local government perceptions of discretion
Although the local government reforms were met with some gloom — particularly among those former parish council members who foresaw immediate political death on 1 April 1970, when the mergers reduced the number of local governments by 80 per cent — there were sincere hopes, notably among former town politicians, that they would mean real decentralization for the new municipalities.

Picard (1983) has interviewed local government leaders and compared their perceptions of the original goals of the reforms with their perceptions of the major effects. Two-thirds saw the primary goal as the provision of more responsibility for policy decisions to subordinate government institutions, that is, decentralization, but only one in seven found that it had been realized. And nearly one-half found that the distance between citizen and government had increased.

Picard conducted his interviews in 1979. When Skovsgaard (1984) conducted his surveys in 1981 and 1982, the criticism was again harsh. About 80 per cent of respondents found that the central government had not foreseen the economic and administrative consequences of the decision to transfer tasks to local government. On the other hand, only one-third felt that too many tasks had been transferred to the localities — and those that were most dissatisfied were those from the smallest municipalities — with fewest resources to manage them. At the same time, it is rural politicians who believe the state mandates too many issues.

These surveys indicate that the rural areas have had some difficulties in coping with the reforms, while the cities have fared better; in political terms because the national parties were dominant there, even before the reforms, and in administrative terms because they have had the capacity to take on new functions. The cities are able to process and use the new instruments provided by central government, whereas the rural areas have not found the need to use such sophisticated instruments for their relatively simple problems (Bogason and Zachariassen, 1984). Rural areas have found their discretion curbed by the developments of the 1970s, but the cities have been more satisfied.

Advice and regulation — two faces of influence
Central agencies have shifted between regulating the details of general legal requirements and supplying detailed advice. However, a more consistent pattern of relationship has been established around contacts between ministries and local government associations, both in general local government matters and in specific policy fields. Almost all initiatives are discussed with the organizations and if agreement is reached during the preparation of a parliamentary bill, it can be safely predicted that parliament's influence will be small.

It is a fact of some significance that Denmark is a small country. Administrators at various levels know one another personally, from university days, conferences and professional meetings. The British tradition of frequently moving civil servants from one position to another is less pronounced in Denmark. Over the past fifteen to twenty years, a fairly small number of people have been the main actors in shaping and developing the reforms, and on many issues — such as the development of planning instruments and budgetary systems — there has been little disagreement on the main principles, in particular on the need to help local government administrators and top politicians to elaborate better decision-making procedures and obtain more structured information for that purpose.

Nonetheless, as we saw above, a measure of dissatisfaction with the regulatory burden is found among many local government actors, in particular those from rural areas. In this respect, there seems to be a gulf between the associations — and their professional staff — and the localities. This dissatisfaction, as well as a general desire to reduce the administrative burdens on local government, led the Department of Administration to review the framework for local government regulation by interviewing state and local officers, and by reviewing and classifying all regulations for 1980 to get a picture of the general regulatory thrust (Administratorsdepartmentet, 1982).

The decision to classify the regulations had several results. The main aim was to regulate the material content of future local government decisions, rather than to influence them through personnel regulation, finance and planning. But the most frequently used instrument was regulation of procedures, often combined with specifications about how services should be delivered, what level should be provided and who should receive the benefits.

If one aim of the reforms of the 1970s was to give local government more discretion, the results of this examination of the intergovernmental regulations are somewhat contradictory. A large majority — 71 per cent — of the regulations were classified as mandatory and binding. Seventy-five per cent were classified as regulating a very specific policy aspect, and 40 per cent as very detailed. A number of local government officers at interview expressed annoyance over the sheer volume of state regulation. The formal status of the rules was considered to be of minor importance — by and large, all regulations were treated as if they were binding. This, of course, added to the administrative burden of local government; in general, state regulations were held to increase local expenditure. Local government officers disagreed about the relevance of the regulations: some found that most were irrelevant to their department; other expressed a desire for regulation of problems that they found pressing.

State administrators agreed that the rationale for regulation was based on a need to update information in the light of new knowledge and experience. This was a view expressed by parliamentary committees, as well as by local authorities themselves. Most central administrators were aware that local authorities lack the capacity to take an overview of their work, although some were studying how to solve this problem

In sum, the general intention of the reforms of the 1970s — to give local government more room for policy making — has not been fulfilled completely, and the Department of Administration is recommending a general simplification of the regulatory system, including some deregulation. The Minister of the Interior has initiated four-year experiments in twenty-two municipalities and five counties that allow them to deviate from regulations within specified policy fields, in so far as equality before the law and the general public health are not jeopardized. In most cases, these experiments were to take place in the 1986–1990 election period. Parliament has authorized the minister to allow deviations from a number of statutory rules. In most cases, the experiments will decentralize budgetary powers to individual institutions. Furthermore, the Minister of Social Affairs has initiated experiments designed to reduce the administrative burden in social case work, partly by suggesting a number of standard rates for social assistance payments.

Limitations on local finance
Local government in Denmark has seven main sources of income. Income tax is charged on the basis of taxable income, in the same way it is by the state, with some technical adjustments. The municipalities assess taxable income on the basis of an elaborate code devised by the state Directorate of Taxes. Each council determines its own rate on the basis of an assessment of financial need and the projections for other sources of revenue. In 1985, the rate varied between 13 and 21 per cent for the municipalities (average 18.5 per cent), and between 8 and 10 per cent for county councils (average 8.7 per cent). Thus local income tax represents about 27.5 per cent of taxable personal income, on average. Other taxes are of little importance. The municipalities get 20 per cent of corporation tax.

Property tax is levied on the basis of an assessment of the value of private land. Assessments are made locally on the basis of recent sales. The rates vary among municipalities in a range from 0 to 5 per cent. All county councils had a state-mandated rate of 1 per cent in 1985.

The block grant is distributed on the basis of the local government's taxable income per capita. In 1985, the block grant amounted to DKr 6 billion for the municipalities and DKr 12 billion for the counties. The block grant has been cut back in recent years — in 1982, it totalled DKr 22 billion. Grants to municipalities have been cut by 50 per cent, but the counties have had a modest increase. The government wishes to cut the block grant further, and in 1986 the municipalities gave up DKr 3 billion. Social expenditure by the municipalities is reimbursed. The percentage is 100 for pensions, 75 for sick pay and 50 for social assistance costs (limited to certain types of expenditure). The social assistance reimbursements will be abolished in 1987 and an equivalent sum added to the block grant of the municipalities.

Charges are fees paid for services such as water and gas, kindergartens and other institutions. These types of income are of increasing importance.

Loans are of little importance to local governments, except for a few that are caught in a financial squeeze. Interest is earned by many councils because they have excess liquidity. This question is discussed in greater detail below.

Table 2 indicated the structure of local government income. Some differences between municipal and county councils that do not show up in the aggregate figures are worth noting. Counties get no reimbursements, whereas these account for 48 per cent of the income of municipal councils. Block grants represent one-quarter of county income, but less than one-tenth of municipal income. Local taxes cover only about 35 per cent of municipal income, but 54 per cent of county revenue. The property tax is of little importance.

The differences in income patterns reflect the reforms of the early 1970s, when most social welfare tasks were transferred to the municipalities, to be paid for through a reimbursement scheme; the hospitals were transferred to the counties, with the introduction of a block grant system. The income pattern of the municipalities from the early 1970s to date shows an increasing reliance on state funds, which have risen from about 55 per cent of income to 58 per cent, with a peak of 60 per cent in 1977.

A state-mandated equalization system is financed entirely by local governments, and consists of transfers among them. The system enables local administrations with below-average taxable income per capita to get 50 per cent of the shortfall, financed by those with above the average. Furthermore, expenditure-creating factors are equalized by the use of variables. By subtracting the actual average expenditure on each inhabitant of all local government areas from the level of spending that a particular municipality or county is estimated to 'need', one gets a figure indicating whether the municipality or county is to receive or pay money in that part of the scheme. A special equalization mechanism is found in the metropolitan area, and there is a state grant for municipalities that are in a particularly bad position.

In 1977, a budgetary reform changed the principles of budgeting and accounting in local government. The measure was prepared over several years by central government and the local government associations. Until 1977, a one-year budget was normal in many municipalities; because budgets comprised net expenditure, real service costs were concealed. Today, local government uses a four-year budget based on standardized categories, so that local budgets are comparable. State and local budgets can then be summed to produce a total public-sector budget.

This reform came in the wake of changes in the grant system. The block grant, with fewer ties on local priorities, was introduced in 1973 to replace categorical grants and conditional reimbursements. The aim was clear enough: to increase the accountability of local government in the budgetary process. The reform in 1979 led to the formulation of the first reliable national budget, and political reaction came quickly when parliament became aware of the rate of growth in local spending. After negotiations with the local government interest organizations, spending limits were introduced that were intended to reduce real growth from 4 per cent in 1980 to 0 in 1984. The ministries were asked to provide advice on ways to manage the cuts, and the local government associations developed more sophisticated methods for examining the components of the budgets, in order to enhance efficiency.

During the 1970s, there had been a continuing common understanding among the central administration and local governments that, in order to ease the implementation of macroeconomic policy, restrictions would occasionally be put on local government fiscal management. But this ad hoc co-operation was formalized from 1979, and local government soon found itself part of a macro-level public-sector resource management policy (Friisberg, 1984). Following the spending limits, in 1983–85 the block grants were cut back by about DKr 10,000 million, and the local authorities were asked not to increase local taxes. In 1984, they were ordered to freeze a centrally estimated excess liquidity of nearly DKr 2,500 million.

For its part, central government has agreed not to initiate any cost-intensive policies, to be implemented by local governments, unless a similar-size cutback option is provided. This is to counter a widespread criticism among local politicians that state regulation is increasing local costs.

The demands for fiscal stringency have meant a fairly rapid shift from growth management to management of the status quo, or even cutbacks in some municipalities. Mouritzen (1974) uses the term 'financial squeeze' to denote municipalities with a fairly high tax rate, poor liquidity and high interest payments. The budgetary behaviour of such municipalities has been such that they have the lowest growth in net spending and the greatest cutback in capital costs, relative to others. Nevertheless, they have suffered the sharpest rise in local taxes and debts.

The changes in financial resources have had unequal consequences for the various local government services. In general, schools and cultural programmes have seen their share of the budget reduced from about 40 to 35 per cent. Growth in service provision has been particularly large in the urban areas, associated as it is with high unemployment rates and welfare assistance payments (Dilling-Hansen, 1984). It is also linked to a heavy demand for day-care institutions for children below school age.

Theorists have discussed the importance of sectoral decision making. Some have argued that, in so far as local politicians and administrators have counterparts at the regional and central levels and can get support from client organizations, they are able to decide their budget with a fairly high degree of autonomy vis-a-vis the finance committee and the municipal council. Danish experience seems to indicate that, in a resource squeeze, the politicians' sectoral priorities are undermined, with party loyalties, indicating a 'system' perspective, becoming relatively more important (Mouritzen, 1982). Budgets are not cut in big lumps, however; budgetary policy makers seem to share an incrementally oriented notion of equal misery all round. It is not the size of the budget per se that catches their eye, rather the relative change in the expenditure on each item.

Access

Party political linkages

The national parties have increased their role in local government politics, although some local lists still exist. From 1920 to 1970, about 60 per cent of all seats were held by national parties. By 1978, the proportion had risen to nearly 90 per cent (Bentzon, 1981). The shift was caused by the reform of 1970, which reduced the total number of seats and created a better basis for party politics in the new enlarged municipalities.

As Table 4 shows, voting patterns are different at county and municipal elections. The three largest parties get more votes in local government polls than at national elections. Two parties — the socialists and the centre-democrats — get fewer votes, and the rest get

TABLE 4
Denmark: support for the major parties in local elections, 1981
(per cent)

	County	Municipality	Parliament
Social Democrats	35.8	34.0	32.9
Radical Party	6.2	4.7	5.1
Conservatives	16.4	16.2	14.5
Socialist Party	6.1	5.7	11.3
Communists	1.9	1.9	1.1
Centre-democrats	1.7	0.9	8.3
Christian Party	1.8	1.2	2.3
Agrarian Party	19.1	17.1	11.3
Left Socialists	2.0	2.5	2.7
Progress Party	7.4	6.3	8.9
Other	1.9	9.5	1.5

Source: Statistisk Arbok, Stockholm, 1983.

roughly the same share. At local elections, special lists play a greater role, taking about 8 per cent of the votes.

Thus, at national and county levels, national parties dominate. In some municipalities, local lists play a significant role: they account for 13 per cent of the mayors, mainly in small towns. It should be emphasized that, in general, local politics is considered different from national politics. A Social Democrat from North Jutland might well disagree on some issues with a party member from Copenhagen. Finally, it should be stressed that, at county and national levels, the electoral system does not favour special lists. Only a municipality can address the particular demands of local policy.

Only a few MPs retain their seats on a local council when elected to parliament. In 1971, 47 per cent were serving, or had previous experience as councillors; the figure dropped to 32 per cent in 1973 (Damgaard, 1977:106) but in 1984 increased to 44 per cent. The workload or party rules prevent most MPs from keeping their seat in a local government; the Social Democrats do not allow national politicians to hold the office of mayor. It is quite common for such politicians to start their political career at the local level, but one cannot infer that all local politicians have a national future in mind. Many have strong local roots.

About one-quarter of leading local politicians have a position in the regional or central party apparatus (Villadsen, 1984). The regional level is more important in this respect than the national — the number of national positions is more limited. An investigation into the frequency of interaction between local, regional and national politicians shows that 70 per cent of leading local politicians have less than one contact a month with the regional level, and 86 per cent have less than one contact with the central level. Social Democrats have more contacts than do right-wing parties.

Local politicians do try to influence decisions taken at the centre that are seen as likely to affect their local area. In a four-year term, much of the time with a Social Democratic government, most members of the local government elite made more than one attempt to lobby through the party channel — 83 per cent of the Social Democrats made two or more attempts. In most cases, the efforts were directed towards making changes in laws and administrative circulars, but quite a few — about 40 per cent — concerned specific issues affecting individual municipalities (Mouritzen, 1984).

Local government associations
Local government interest groups have existed for many years. Before 1970, three organizations represented the lowest tier: one for the towns, one for the parishes and one for the urban parishes. These were

merged with the reforms of 1970, and the new organization, the Kommunernes Landsforening (KL) was from the start dominated by the former municipal organization in terms of staff and leadership. The county councils have their own organization, the Amtsradsforeningen (ARF).

Both organizations have grown in size and importance in the 1970s and 1980s — especially the KL, which has a large staff. It is at the centre of a network of organizations that render services to local government, including a large computer centre, a chemical destruction plant, an accounting firm and, in collaboration with the ARF, a training school for local politicians and staff. Both organizations act as lobbyists for local interests, partly as mentioned earlier, by negotiating changes to bills at the draft stage, and partly by trying to influence the committees which discuss the content of the bills during their passage through parliament. Of equal importance is the associations' role in implementing legislation. The KL and the ARF both offer local expertise, information and advice, and help to give the ministries' work enhanced legitimacy. Furthermore, they influence public opinion through their own journals and by acting as information centres for the press. In their daily work, they help local government officers by offering advice over the telephone, through general information services and by providing advice on how to interpret legislation. The KL also runs a public-service consultancy agency, offering help in analysing local government policy problems, planning techniques and organizational design.

In addition the KL plays an important role as the secretariat for the state commission that regulates career structures in local government. Although the roles are formally divided, most local politicians identify the KL with the commission, and its role in this respect has attracted some criticism (Christensen, 1984); however, most members are fairly satisfied with its work. A recent rebellion among Copenhagen county municipalities over the redistribution of the block grant — a protest accepted by the KL — led to the formulation of a new principle for representation on KL's board.

The greatest potential for influencing central government clearly lies in the daily interaction among permanent officials. But a few local politicians have good opportunities to influence ministers. These are the members of the associations' boards, in particular the chairmen. They are frequently interviewed by the press and they have ready access to any minister involved in local government affairs. Unless the minister and the chairman are members of the same political party, such contacts are, however, of a fairly formal nature. This is not to say that the associations work through party political channels. On the contrary, they make great efforts to present the balance of feeling within local government and explicitly to disregard party differences.

Within certain policy fields, there are special organizations of both politicians and administrators channelling the interests of local government to the centre. This is done through formal meetings, such as annual conferences, and by the release of policy statements from the board of the particular association — mostly on the politicians' side. The administrators are more diplomatic in public, but very efficient away from the public gaze because of personal links with their counterparts at the centre; central and local officials may have been at university together, may have worked next to one another in the same organization, or be personal friends. Such influence, of course, works in both directions — from the local to the central level and vice versa. There is no doubt that many initiatives have been developed in response to general agreement among the members of the political/administrative/intergovernmental network. Where disagreement does occur, the associations are able to influence the substance of the decisions quite extensively, as long as they are in agreement among themselves.

Conclusion:
current trends in central–local relations
Any assessment of trends in central–local relations in Denmark must focus on the comprehensive reforms of the 1970s and their consequences for local government — and for central government as well. One key word is consolidation. Local authorities were merged in order to secure greater viability in economic terms: broader tax bases and more professional local administration. At the same time, economic responsibility was enhanced by a reduction in categorical grants in favour of a block grant and/or partial reimbursement scheme. Finally, reforms aimed at enhancing public visibility were introduced: local government was mandated to formulate policy in many sectors by preparing and implementing plans that were to be made public. In addition, public debate was to be stimulated by the physical planning procedures, which gave wide access to the public.

Central–local relations before 1970 were characterized primarily by a complex system of categorical grants and reimbursements, elaborate standards regulating even minor decisions, control of the legality of the decisions and often mandatory approval by a central authority before a local decision could be implemented. The 1970 reforms had as a target a reduction in the number and scope of centrally determined standards, enabling local government to formulate local policy and bear the economic consequences of that policy. Central–local relations would, in these terms, change into a system of dialogue, based on central policy statements and advisory activities, local policy formulation and implementation, followed by central review of the consequences of local decisions on the national scale.

In economic terms, local government has increasingly been made part of a national fiscal policy aiming at, first, a reduction in aggregate demand and, second, a reduction in the growth of the public sector — plus, in recent years, a reduction in its absolute size. The reforms of the budgetary and accounting systems have helped to achieve these goals by enhancing the quality of information about local activities available to central policy makers. The role of the central agencies has changed into one of giving advice on how to implement the cuts. Ironically, this advice is much sought after by the local authorities, whereas the advice of the 1970s on service quality was strongly criticized. It appears that many local authorities were unable to distinguish between central advice and central mandate: the general reaction at the local level was that any central statement was a mandate. The role of the state in local government finance has been increased, in monetary terms, at the municipality level because of increases in social expenditure, which attract 50 per cent central government funding. In the block grant schemes, the role of central government has been decreasing, as it has in the equalization measures.

In terms of function, local government — above all, the county level — has increased in importance in the past fifteen years. One important goal of the reforms was to enhance responsibility by abolishing intermunicipal co-operation and crossjurisdictional service delivery, and by reducing the degree of substitution among service agencies by consolidation, in particular in the social sector. The disappearance of categorical grants has reduced the impetus towards issue networks or 'iron triangles' found in other countries because there is no 'budgetary spine', but sectoral politics is still found to some degree, furthered by the structure of central government, the committee structure in local government and special interest organizations. In times of cutback, however, the influence of sectoral politics appears to decrease. The general goal of social effectiveness has clearly been reached in so far as public services are widely used. The goal of increased efficiency appears also to be one that is largely being met, but it remains under threat. For example, municipalities with relatively low youth unemployment allocate more to employment schemes than do those with high unemployment. This is perhaps an indication that large-scale problems receive comparatively little attention in the political process: minor, but visible, difficulties offer greater rewards in local politics.

The discretion pendulum has swung several times during the past fifteen years. In the era of consolidation, local authorities had extensive freedom to formulate their own policies within sectors, but many were probably not prepared for this freedom, in terms of staff and professional expertise. In addition, traditional local politicians were unwilling to abandon their influence on questions of detail that they should have been prepared to delegate. As a result, the number of state regulations outlining the principles of enabling legislation grew progressively, and after some years local governments found themselves in a regulatory maze. Today, a second period of deregulation is being initiated, and experiments have been started to find the acceptable limits of local discretion. There are substantial variations in service output, and it is hardly the aim of central government to reduce such variation. Instead, the idea is to facilitate local choice through planning and budgetary techniques, and the provision of information on the costs and benefits of various service options. This way of influencing local decision making is alone in close collaboration with the local government associations.

These organizations are undoubtedly the main vehicles by which local government gains access to central government, and particularly to the departments and directorates concerned with implementing the local government reforms. The associations are engaged in drafting parliamentary acts — and in preparing administrative circulars and advisory information, work in which party politics plays a small role. Issues affecting changes in local government have been effectively depoliticized. However, party channels still operate as a means of articulating the problems of individual localities and sometimes as a means of influencing the centre on broader issues. Above all, the present government's fiscal stringency has created tensions between right and left wing parties, particularly over social policy.

In sum, then, trends run counter to one another. In the late 1970s regulation of local activities was increasing: deregulation has been introduced in policy terms. At the same time, however, central government is trying to squeeze local government in financial terms, thus curbing local initiatives and forcing cutbacks in other policy fields.

5

Britain

Michael J. Goldsmith and Edward C. Page

Introduction:
the British dual polity
England's tradition of local self-government has long been admired
by its European neighbours (Redlich and Hirst, 1958). Even the fact
that Britain has local government rather than local administration, as
implied in the French concept of *administration locale* or the German
kommunale Selbstverwaltung, has been regarded as significant by
some observers (Gremion, 1970). Consequently, it may appear
surprising that this basic principle appears to be under such great
challenge in contemporary Britain, especially since 1979. Since that
time, local authorities have been told individually how much they
should spend. The injunction to cut spending has been reinforced
through the progressive escalation of the penalties for not doing so;
from reduced grant entitlement to actual grant reduction, to setting
upper limits on the revenue that can be raised through local taxation.
Councils have been forced to sell council houses, prohibited from
spending all the proceeds from these sales, face limitations on their
ability to shape urban transport systems through further
deregulation, and have faced further restrictions in terms of choosing
which contractors should carry out capital projects. Moreover, the
government has chosen to abolish some of the local authorities that it
dislikes — the Greater London Council and the metropolitan counties
— and replace them with non-elected boards.

One must be cautious, however, in describing such changes as
marking a complete discontinuity with the pattern of local self-
government that, arguably, prevailed until the mid-1970s. The aim of
this chapter is to show how the developments of the 1980s are related
to the earlier pattern. Above all, local self-government in Britain was
based on the concept of 'dual polity' (Bulpitt, 1983). This idea refers
to the separation of central and local government that has been noted
in a number of studies of British local government (Ashford, 1982).
British national political elites, so the thesis argues, had traditionally
shown little interest in the more mundane activity of municipal
government. In order to relieve themselves of this task they delegated,
or rather failed to appropriate for themselves, large areas of state
services to the local authorities. In particular, the authorities were
given responsibility for fulfilling a wide range of state functions and

were allowed a high degree of discretion in delivering local services. In turn, central elites became relatively unencumbered by demands for central intervention in local services — a position congruent with their desire to relieve the pressure to become embroiled in unglamorous 'low politics' so that they might devote their attention to issues of 'high politics', such as foreign affairs, defence and taxation. As a result, the desire to remain independent of local political pressures limited the degree of access between local and national political elites.

This paper explores the dual polity concept from three perspectives. First, it discusses functional allocation as one of the thesis's characteristics. Second, it shows how much discretion — another of the concept's major features — local authorities have in different services. Third, it shows how local self-government in the dual polity isolated local from central politicians and created indirect patterns of central–local access. The changes in central–local relations since 1979 underline the weakness of the particular forms of access that developed under the dual polity. Yet at the same time, these changes appear to be beginning to alter the political relationships of access between central and local government.

The functional basis of the dual polity in Britain

Local government in Britain is understood to comprise the forty-seven non-metropolitan counties, thirty-six metropolitan districts, 334 non-metropolitan districts of England and Wales (outside London), the Inner London Education Authority, the thirty-two London boroughs and the City of London, and the nine regional, three island and fifty-three district authorities in Scotland. This chapter largely excludes examination of the local government system in Northern Ireland, where the twenty-six district councils have, since reorganization in 1971, very few remaining functional tasks (Birrell and Murie, 1980).

As the dual polity thesis suggests, local government in Britain has responsibility for a wide range of government functions. This can best be quantified by examining the proportion of total public resources devoted to local government. Following Rose's (1985a) discussion of the three major resources of government — laws, money and manpower — local government consumes a large portion of government resources. Page's (1983) study of local government legislation shows that 28 per cent of laws passed by the House of Commons between 1970 and 1979 affected local government either directly or indirectly. Local government is responsible for 42 per cent of total public capital expenditure and 27 per cent of current spending; a total of 28 per cent of total capital plus current expenditure. Moreover, local government in Britain employs 38 per cent of public sector manpower (Rose, 1985b).

Local government expenditure and manpower has increased as a proportion of the public total since the end of the Second World War. In the early 1950s, the authorities accounted for 26 per cent of total expenditure and 23 per cent of total public sector employment. This rise in local government's share of government resources has taken place despite the fact that it has lost control of some important services since 1945; responsibility for municipal electricity and gas supplies, and hospitals, and cash assistance to the poor and unemployed was taken away in the immediate postwar period. In the 1970s, the local authorities lost the responsibility for residual health services (mainly health visitors and health clinics) that they had retained after the creation of the National Health Service in 1948, as well as for water (except in Scotland). These losses have been more than offset, in financial and manpower terms, by the expansion of the more traditional local services and the development of newer ones such as personal social services (see Newton and Sharpe, 1984).

Table 1 gives a breakdown of the major services of local government in Britain. Largest, in terms of manpower and expenditure, is the education service. Local authorities in Britain are responsible for building, maintaining, staffing and equipping nursery, primary and secondary schools. In addition, they are responsible for higher and further education colleges, teacher-

TABLE 1
England: local authority manpower and expenditure, by service, 1984

Service	% of total expenditure	% of total manpower
Education	31.2	35.9
Housing	20.3	2.3
Police	6.7	6.4
Social services	6.6	8.8
Highways	5.4	a
Passenger transport	2.4	0.7
Planning	2.2	0.8
Refuse collection and disposal	1.7	1.6
Fire	1.5	1.6
Leisure and recreation	1.4	3.1
Libraries and museums	1.1	1.3
Environmental health	0.9	0.8
Other	18.6	36.7
Total	100.0	100.0

a = included with others
Source: Department of the Environment, *Local Authority Financial Statistics, 1983–84*, London: HMSO, 1986.

training colleges and polytechnics. The only significant sector of education for which central government has direct responsibility is the university sector and the Scottish 'central institutions', equivalent to the polytechnics in England and Wales. Even here, local government is responsible for distributing grants to students in the tertiary sector.

Housing is the second most important local government function, in expenditure terms, although relatively low in manpower. In England, 31 per cent of households rent from public authorities, mainly those of local government. In Scotland, the majority of households — 55 per cent — rents from the public sector. The bulk of current local housing spending — 63 per cent — is taken up with servicing the debts incurred in house building and maintenance. Local authorities also offer housing improvement grants to private homeowners. The next largest functional service, in spending terms, comprises labour-intensive personal social services, which include social casework, and residential and day care for children and the elderly, but relatively little by way of cash transfers — only some limited functions of cash assistance for families with children in danger. Police services are only marginally smaller in expenditure terms: London's Metropolitan Police force is run directly by the Home Office.

In almost all the categories listed in Table 1, apart from passenger transport, recreation and highways, local government is the sole provider of services, with central government having almost no service delivery functions. Central government in Britain is, as Sharpe (1978) describes it, 'non-executant'. In fact, central government organizations themselves administer relatively few functions; apart from the armed forces, central ministries proper employ only 15 per cent of all public workers. Local government in Britain has a relatively wide range of functions that constitutes an important portion of total public-sector resources in terms of finance, laws and manpower; it has considerable discretion over how it provides these services, with the exception of education and the police.

Local discretion in the dual polity
It may appear incongruous to talk of substantial local discretion in a polity in which parliamentary sovereignty is the main pillar of the constitution and, as a result, the status of local government is governed by the doctrine of ultra vires, which is understood to mean that 'local authorities have no powers except such as defined by statute' (Clarke, 1939:11). The constitutional–legal status of local government implies a highly pervasive legal influence by central government over the local authorities, above all by the executive, which dominates Parliament. Local government discretion in service

delivery is based on three elements of the legal constrains upon it: the degree of discretion allowed local authorities by defining their actions in terms of permissive legislation or through mandates that leave much to their own interpretation; the absence of a sophisticated system of 'enforcement inspection', scrutiny that enables central government to detect and penalize breaches of statutory provisions; and the relatively wide scope for local revenue raising, but not borrowing. It is primarily the third element that has come under attack from the Conservative government elected in 1979. Although the impact of the rate-capping legislation on local decision making is likely to be extremely wide-ranging, the other two features of discretion — arguably even more important than local revenue raising, on the grounds that discretion still persists in capital projects for which central approval has been required since the early nineteenth century — have not changed quite so dramatically (Schulz, 1948).

Central government constraints on the discretion of local authorities in the provision of local services emerged in the early nineteenth century as a result of three main developments. The first was the initiation of a coherent system of local government, in contrast to the previous patchwork of local bodies, following the Municipal Corporations Act of 1835, which gave urban areas units of government to which powers could be attributed; the practice of using general, as opposed to private, legislation for public services becomes more visible after the 1840s (Keith-Lucas, 1977). Second, the conscious efforts of social reformers, above all in public health, produced policy proposals that sought to subject local authorities to central direction — to coerce them into caring for the health of their citizens. This approach is especially associated with the Secretary to the Poor Law Commissioners, Sir Edwin Chadwick (Gutchen, 1961). Third, although the Chadwickian approach to local government declined in importance later in the nineteenth century, the grant system, originally devised to remove the financial burdens of local service provision from agricultural ratepayers, became recognized by parliament and the executive as a tool that could be used to influence the shape of local services.

However, the expansion of public services within the localities did not generally resemble the pattern of local adoption following central initiation. Many services developed as a result of permissive general legislation, or the acquisition by individual localities of statutory permission to undertake activities through local Acts of Parliament (Keith-Lucas, 1977). Scarrow (1971) documents initiatives by local authorities that ended up as general legislation. Swann (1972) shows how the central decision to provide insulin for diabetics was prompted by local practice; the building control functions Liverpool council acquired through local act in 1849 became an important influence on later private and general legislation. Griffith (1927:207) observed that:

> especially after 1890 there was an important increase in the number of adoptive and permissive acts whereby Parliament sought to make available powers adequate to the needs of towns. The list was a long one and represented only one phase of a well-marked later trend towards the fostering of local government.

Chester (1951:93) suggests that the importance of local initiative to national policy persisted until well after the Second World War:

> The impetus for the postwar housing drive came as much, if not more, from the local authorities as from the Minister of Health and his officials. Most of the educational ideas embodied in the Education Act of 1944 were strongly supported and had indeed been advocated for some time by the Local Educational Authorities.

The local origins of many local public services were thus reflected both in the nature of the legislation itself, which defined powers and duties nationally, as well as in a general approach to local government that tended to include substantial scope for local discretion.

Of course, the general principle that local discretion should be preserved was not uniformly applied in legislation for major public services, some of which developed within a statutory context that granted greater discretion than others received. It is not possible to offer a detailed description of the nature of statutory constraint and discretion across different services for a variety of reasons: there are literally thousands of items of legislation (that is, statutes and regulations, statutory instruments and orders) affecting local government; even the major services can be broken down into a number of discrete activities (for example, housing into tenant selection, maintenance, building control, and so on) that make detailed description a lengthy exercise. Legal provisions themselves are frequently imprecise, so that it is difficult to appreciate their implications in the abstract, especially if they have not been tested in the courts. Furthermore, to discuss the implications of statutory constraints implies an ability to specify the counter-factual conditions that would prevail in the absence of the legislation. However, it is possible to offer a broad characterization of the those statutory constraints that have the most important implications for local service delivery, and to point to major areas of service delivery not subject to centrally defined legislation (Page, 1982; INLOGOV, 1983).

Education is a service in which the statutory framework has an important effect on the nature of the service provided. Local authorities are mandated to provide education for children of school age, between five and sixteen years. Education at preschool level has not been mandatory since 1980, although the status of higher education as a mandatory/non-mandatory service is unclear. Nevertheless, for the bulk of education spending (62 per cent of current and 66 per cent of capital expenditure is devoted to primary and secondary schools) the service is mandated, as is the clientele for whom it is provided. The importance of this mandatory requirement is seen in the close statistical relationship between per capita spending on education and the number of children of school age within a locality noted in studies of local spending (Boaden, 1971). School buildings and playing fields, teacher qualifications and the length of school terms represent the other major statutory constraints on local authorities in the provision of education. Since 1969, staffing levels have not been subject to uniform statutory standards, and, with the exception of religious instruction, there are no statutory conditions governing the school curriculum.

Housing is not a service mandated to local authorities. The 1977 Housing (Homeless Persons) Act defined local authorities' obligation to house the homeless, but it allowed considerable scope for local interpretation of 'homelessness' and has been widely circumvented by the authorities (Birkinshaw, 1982). Nor are the standards of repair and maintenance to be met by public housing particularly exacting; the authorities are obliged to review the housing in their area, yet are under no strict obligation to repair or demolish even their own stock that is 'below tolerable standard', even though the criteria for making such judgements, in both public and private sectors, are statutorily defined. The limitations on local discretion emerge if the authority decides to start a building or maintenance project. Local government capital expenditure projects must largely be approved by central government. Despite the formal abandonment of the housing cost yardsticks and the Parker–Morris standards in the Housing Investment Programme (HIP) approach, which was intended (among other things) to give local authorities greater freedom to decide the nature of their housing programmes, cost factors are still included in the criteria used to grant central approval for capital projects (for a good discussion of HIPs, see Leather, 1983). Moreover, the system has been used to impose a greater degree of positive influence over local authority housing spending through the application of relatively uniform criteria of 'need' for capital expenditure, and through the use of capital approvals to encourage and penalize those authorities that fail to conform to other central government objectives, for example rent levels and the renovation of old stock. Of course, the local authority is also subject to building control regulations. In housing management, rent levels are not statutorily defined (a short-lived statutory fixing of rents in 1972 provoked one of the few nationally publicized central–local conflicts before the 1980s, the Clay Cross affair).

Of the remaining services, the only one in which relatively well-defined central constraints make the scope for local influence relatively small is the police service, in which staffing levels are subject to central approval, as are equipment, uniform, wage levels and even, according to the 1970 Police Regulations, the 'private life of police officers'. Regan (1966) suggested that the police service constitutes 'an extreme example of central control over local authority staff.' In the remaining services defined in Table 1, the local authorities have to enforce a variety of laws, for example in the areas of environmental health and planning; the legal framework is best seen as offering a variety of powers, duties and procedures that the 'street level' bureaucrats, planners and environmental health officers, as well as the collective decision-making body of the local authority, can enforce, rather than as a strict constraint that defines a more or less 'national' planning and environmental health service, as found in education and the police.

Local authorities are obliged to repair and maintain local roads, yet standards of repair and maintenance are not statutorily defined, apart from the legal requirement to make roads passable. For leisure and recreation and public transport, the authorities enjoy mainly permissive legislation, while for libraries, and fire and civil defence services, they are mandated to provide adequate services, although the criteria for adequacy are not defined.

One crude general indicator of the level of discretion enjoyed by local authorities over different services can be found in the variation in per capita spending for those services (for a discussion of the limitations of this measure, see Boaden [1971], and Newton and Sharpe [1984]). However, local government reorganization makes the long-term examination of this measure difficult. Even so, Table 2 largely confirms expectations about the exercise of discretion over per capita spending on local services: the coefficient of variation, that is, the standard deviation divided by the mean, is low in education (0.8 in 1982) and police services (0.08). It is higher in services such as housing (0.77), planning (0.60), recreation (0.64) and public health (0.39), where the statutory provisions do not appear to impose strict limitations on the type of service any one authority provides. Social services vary relatively less widely than the others, suggesting the importance of statutory obligations, above all in childcare functions. Only highways (0.22) and libraries (0.15) appear to be more uniform services than the brief examination of statutory obligations would suggest. Nevertheless, the figures offer broad confirmation for the suggestion that central government legislation imposes a strong constraint on the nature of local education and police services, with the localities enjoying considerable discretion in the nature of the other services they provide, even if these are law-intensive enforcement services such as environmental health.

TABLE 2
England: Coefficients of variation in local services, 1957–82

Service	1957	1961	1965	1969	1973	1982*
Education	0.11	0.10	0.09	0.10	0.10	0.08
Police	n/a	0.11	0.16	0.16	0.19	0.08
Social services	n/a	0.23	0.25	0.29	0.20	0.15
Libraries	n/a	0.23	0.25	0.29	0.26	0.15
Highways	n/a	0.20	0.21	0.21	0.20	0.22
Public health	n/a	0.26	0.33	0.23	0.32	0.39
Recreation	0.52	0.48	0.50	0.43	0.40	0.64
Planning	n/a	0.98	n/a	0.71	0.70	0.60
Housing	n/a	0.36	0.43	0.50	0.61	0.77

*Figures for non-metropolitan areas only; earlier years are for county boroughs.

Of course, statutory provisions are not the only source of central influence over the discretion of local politicians in service provision. Central government also seeks to advise local authorities over the way in which services are provided. It does so primarily through the use of circulars, manuals and other documents that seek to exhort, encourage and disseminate good practice. For example, although there are no statutory requirements for social work coverage (such as quotas for available places in homes for old people, number of day care and residential places for children), or technical standards for road maintenance, these matters constitute important topics for central government advice. Such advice abounds within local government services, and some generalizations about its effects are possible.

First, there is no general predisposition to accept central government advice merely because it comes from central government. Unlike a system such as exists in France, many local government professions in Britain have a self-image of expertise. Moreover, there are professional sources for disseminating advice and good practice, which means central government hardly has a monopoly on advice. Indeed, much of the general advice to local authorities on technical matters is generally 'cleared' by, if not drawn up in conjuction with, local authority professional groups. When central government issues 'grandmotherly' advice, local authorities can and do generally ignore it (Association of County Councils, 1980; Page, 1982).

Second, circulars and other forms of advice can be an important means of influence if groups within local government use them to bargain among themselves. Laffin's (1982) study of highway engineers shows how this group sought to introduce advisory codes for highway repair and maintenance partly in order to enhance their political importance and to claim a larger share of the budget for their service.

Third, circulars and advice become important when they are formally or informally tied to other forms of influence. The most obvious example is when a circular is interpreted as an expression of the secretary of state's discretionary powers; for example, in Scotland the legal obligation to provide regional reports was communicated to local authorities through a circular. The impact of such efforts may be buttressed by less direct means. One comprises the definition of standards that might be accepted in a court of law or some other arena (for example, by an auditor) as a definitive interpretation of the statutes. Although most circulars interpreting statutes contain a disclaimer to the effect that interpretation is a matter for the courts, they have in the past been used successfully as a means to establish the legal obligations of local authorities. Another is through tying receipt of money or statutory approval to compliance with recommended standards, as in the provision of grants for police services or the old system of approving housing projects that should, at least, conform to the guidance given in housing cost yardsticks.

The second component of local government discretion is the absence of a developed territorial structure within the central state organization that can enforce legislation. The regional offices of central government departments do not primarily fill this function, since they generally act as gatekeepers, or local officers with limited discretionary powers to approve local capital expenditure projects or provide grants for urban projects, rather than as routine inspectors of local authorities more generally (Hogwood and Keating, 1982). There is a variety of central government inspectors, but as Rhodes (1981:222) shows, those concerned with scrutinizing whether the legal requirements of local government are being met — 'enforcement inspectors' — have tended to 'move away from strict enforcement and detection and towards advice and protection.'

Perhaps the most important of the enforcement inspectorates for local government is the auditor. Until 1980, when the audit arrangements were changed, the district auditor was empowered to ensure the correctness of accounting practices, and that the management of accounts, receipts and payments was legal; another role was to encourage value for money. The auditor was important in the detection and prevention of fraud but rarely got involved in issues concerning the legality of particular policies (Doig, 1984). In the nineteenth century auditors had sought to adopt this more active role, but for most of the twentieth century made only sporadic appearances in debates about the legality of some types of expenditure, for example the case of Poplar in the 1920s and Clay Cross in the 1970s, (Robson, 1925). In 1980, the government set up the Audit Commission, a quango, to replace the office of district auditor, and gave it the express mandate to produce, under ministerial direction if necessary, studies of value for money across different services. Fears that the arrival of the Audit Commission heralded a new phase in government audit, with the extension of auditors' powers through direct application of value for money (for example, by disallowing expenditure that was not considered value for money), and through its subservience to central government, appear to have been misplaced. But the fact that the value-for-money reports are as advisory in nature as the older district auditors' reports, and that the Audit Commission has produced reports critical of central policies towards local finance, has served to dampen such fears.

The third element of the discretion allowed local authorities relates to control over local income. This element has traditionally been the weakest, and has suffered the sharpest reversals in the 1980s. The financial discretion of local authorities, at least from the 1960s to the 1980s, rested largely on their ability to determine local tax levels and on their receipt of funds from the centre in the form of a block grant, unrelated to levels or standards of service provision. British local authorities are not free, as are many municipalities in the United States, to choose their tax base. They are dependent on ratable values, a notional calculation of the annual rental value of property, upon which they levy a percentage. Moreover, they are unable to engage in general revaluation of property; the timing of revaluations is a matter for central government, and the last to be done in England and Wales was carried out in 1973.

Some local services, such as transport, housing and police, are subject to specific grants from central government, but the bulk of such transfers comes in the form of a block grant, introduced in stages in 1888, 1929 and, most important, 1958. The main characteristic of the block grant is that it allows local authorities to use central finance to support any of their services, even those that are supported by specific grants from central government.

The erosion of both these bases for local financial discretion has been documented elsewhere (Goldsmith and Newton, 1984). The block grant principle remains, despite proposals for a specific education grant mooted but abandoned in the early 1980s. Yet the grant system has undergone substantial changes in the 1980s. First, the government has identified spending levels (Grant Related Expenditure Assessments) and targets for each local authority which it can — and has — used to penalize those that it regards as overspending. Second, in producing these figures, central government makes assumptions about spending on individual services within the locality that could serve as a basis for greater intervention in spending on local services by particular authorities. This possibility has yet to be realized.

Perhaps the most important single measure eroding local discretion over finance is the 1984 Rates Act, known as the 'rate-capping' legislation. According to the provisions of this law, the Secretary of

State for the Environment can identify individual authorities that overspend and set upper limits for their rates in the following year (as he did in 1984 and 1985), or set general rate levels across the whole of England and Wales. This has the potential to limit total local expenditure, since spending and income must balance.

If the rate-capping legislation remains a permanent feature of central–local relations (which may be doubted, in view of the political problems likely to be encountered in applying it — a foretaste of which was provided by the struggle between the Environment Minister and Liverpool City Council in 1984), and if to this is added the existing capacity of central government to influence capital standing, it may be seen that the financial discretion of local government is narrowing. Without seeking to underestimate the crucial importance of the changes in central–local finance that have taken place since the late 1970s, those changes do not, of course, mean that local financial discretion is now non-existent. Local authorities' capital expenditure is generally affected, but not determined, by central approvals; the authorities overspent by 7 per cent in 1983–84, in contrast with the high levels of underspend — equally irritating to central government — of earlier years. Similarly, the power to fix the maximum spending levels of a few or even all local authorities does not totally remove their ability to set rates and determine spending within that limit, and to decide spending priorities across a wide range of services.

Patterns of access:
the political basis of the dual polity
Bulpitt's dual polity thesis suggests that, in political terms, local government elites have little influence over national policy-making processes, even in areas where their concerns may be directly affected. How is it possible for such a low level of participation in national policy making to persist when so many nationally important services are, in fact, delivered by local government? Bulpitt's argument suggests that the status and role of local political actors in national policy-making processes is a subordinate one. It refers to a dominance by the centre of national policy-making processes that affect local government. Apart from the sovereignty of Parliament, this political subordination is based on two main features of the relationships among politicians of the centre and the locality; first, the absence of substantial interpenetration between national and local politicians, and, second, the latter's low status, and the dominance of national priorities and strategies within the major parties.

This lack of interpenetration between national and local politics is not primarily a function of the near-absence, in Britain, of members of Parliament (MPs) with some background or experience in local government. Figures show that 36 per cent of MPs had some sort of local government experience in 1951 and 35 per cent in 1979. Mackenzie (1951:355) states that the figures for councillors as MPs do not illustrate his major point about the peculiarity of local government in the British political system — that 'there has hardly been a squeak of protest in the Commons, on either side of the House, on the numerous occasions since 1945 when issues of national policy have led to a reduction in local powers.' This aspect of British central–local relations is discussed by Sharpe (1982) as part of the 'puzzle of territorial inequality' and is a feature of central–local political relations to which Ashford (1982), and Gyford and James (1983), among others, have drawn attention.

In part, this separation results from the fact that local political elites did not need to develop close party political contacts with central government because they operated within a statutory framework that offered relatively high levels of discretion; central approval for matters great and small was not always required. The status and expertise of local officials meant that, unlike in France, local politicians and administrators were independent of the technical expertise and advice of central officials. Nevertheless, the direct contacts that existed with central government (frequently surrounding the need to obtain statutory approval for loans and projects) tended to be dominated by those made through the bureaucratic channel — local and central officials (Griffith, 1966).

Yet there were also more fundamental political reasons for the somewhat limited access to central government that had persisted since the expansion of local government from the early nineteenth century on (one of the basic premises of British urban history is that local politics was distinct from national politics). For most of the first three quarters of the nineteenth century, the cost of local services represented a minimal drain on central resources, with central government grants amounting to less than 10 per cent of all local expenditure. Local taxes (67 per cent in 1868) and user charges (29 per cent) were the main ways in which local services were financed at that time. But from the 1888 local government reform on, this pattern changed, as the authorities became most-purpose bodies and acquired a wider range of functions. The evidence suggests that the separation of central and local political elites persisted after 1888; much was left to the locality, and a few worthy members of local elites were rewarded with seats in Parliament, but little else. In this sense, the famous names from local government, such as the Chamberlain family of Birmingham, were exceptional, because those who left the locality for the central parliamentary arena rarely reached cabinet office.

Bulpitt (1983) argues that this separation of national from local politics arose from the centre's desire and need to keep the periphery or localities quiet, leaving it free to pursue issues of 'high' politics, while the local authorities dealt with peripheral matters, or 'low' politics. They could deal with parish matters, and the local elites who ran them could be trusted to ensure that such matters as they did deal with could, by and large, be kept off the national agenda. Such an arrangement worked well for most of the nineteenth century, with local authorities increasing their powers largely by promoting private acts of Parliament that were carefully examined and approved by the appropriate parliamentary committee. Indeed, when the centre did seek to impose its view of the services that local authorities should be providing, or how much they should cost, this provoked great resentment among the authorities, as experience in the fields of poor law administration, public health and the development of the audit system demonstrate. While the authorities were getting on with the job, it was easier, in political terms, to leave them to it, and not seek to impose the sort of constraints that would bring them to the doors of Westminster and Whitehall.

The interwar years are also the period in which local government more and more came to be dominated by what Lee (1962) has called the 'public person', as distinct from the 'social leader' who dominated in the nineteenth century; local administration fell into the hands of those who owed their status and position in society to what they did in local government, whether as councillor or officer, rather than to their social position. Again, like the petty nobility that dominated county government prior to reform, such people could, by and large, be trusted to manage the localities, and not use their local government position to pursue political aspirations above their station (Hintze, 1962).

There were, of course, some political contacts between central and local politicians, especially in the old county boroughs, the provincial cities that largely returned Labour MPs. But the nature of these links underlines the nature of the separation of national from local politics; a contemporary observer wrote: 'where party loyalty is not involved, local loyalty is so strong as to be decisive' (Mackenzie, 1951: 355). The most visible national–local contacts were found in matters such as boundary changes — a vital concern for national and local office-holders alike.

In the absence of a general pattern of direct political contact between local and central government, relationships tended to be dominated by national associations of local politicians. In 1956, the Minister of Housing and Local Government referred to the local authority associations as 'part of the constitution, with hardly a piece of legislation being passed on which they are not consulted.' The associations became an important element in policy formulation, but it is important not to exaggerate their actual influence; as Mackenzie (1954:352) argued: 'the associations are less powerful on greater matters than small.' First, the associations often could not agree among themselves on major policy issues, as the 1963 reform of London's government shows (Smallwood, 1965). This has been a traditional feature of the associations (Griffith, 1927). Second, there emerged a variety of functional interest groups centred round the interests of clients and advocates of services; the permanent local officials who provided these services interacted with the functional divisions in central government to produce what have come to be referred to as 'policy communities'. Individual localities, especially those with a record of good practice or innovation, retained access to the centre, but it came largely through professional, officer-based networks (indeed, reputations for good practice and innovation were generated within these same networks), rather than via some political channel.

The separation of national from local politics is the first major characteristic of patterns of access in the dual polity. The second such characteristic, the subordination of local to national party strategy and priority, is related to the first, and quantitative evidence for it is equally hard to provide. As with the population as a whole, within the Conservative and Labour parties there developed a 'cultural disdain' for local government (Greenwood, 1982). Only in the early years of the Labour Party was municipal office seen as a route to national political office and power; many leading Labour politicians in the 1920s and 1930s served as councillors before moving on to Parliament. The best-known example is Herbert Morrison, the formidable representative of London interests. Yet local office was seen largely as an apprenticeship for higher things, rather than reflecting a belief that the possession of municipal power was, in itself, important. Bulpitt (1982) argues that:

> after the first taste of national power in 1924 the Labour Party increasingly perceived politics in terms of gaining power at the centre: the working class was to be dragged into a primarily bourgeois-conceived utopia, not via Durham or South Wales, but through the traditional corridors of Westminster and Whitehall. For the Conservative leaders, Labour was a far better territorial opponent than the Liberal Party. The Parliamentary Labour Party could be relied upon not to play territorial cards. On the other hand, at the local level, Labour provided sound, if often dreary and pompous collaborative 'chaps' to manage the less salubrious areas of Britain. But even where there was an overlap of national and local political experience, the principle of isolation of national from local political spheres was maintained; local politicians tended to lose community ties once elected to Parliament.

Further evidence about the low status of municipal office comes from the process of candidate selection within the major parties. Office-holders in local government do not appear particularly favoured over other candidates in local party selection of MPs. As Mackenzie (1951; 1954) argues, the 'carpetbagging' system of candidate selection serves to weaken further any links between national and local office, and demonstrates the lack of status of local politicians within the party. This point is demonstrated in Rush's (1969) study of MP selection between 1950 and 1966. First, a direct local connection with the constituency (as opposed to some form of political activity within the larger geographical area) was held by only 22 per cent of the candidates of ruling Conservative parties, 23 per cent of ruling Labour parties with trade-union sponsored candidates and 25 per cent of non-union-sponsored Labour Party candidates. Second, any advantages accruing from local government come from experience of local administration (not necessarily within the constituency) rather than office, although such experience is more common among candidates of opposition than ruling parties. Local government experience demonstrates a willingness to conduct an electoral campaign or, in some circumstances, that a potential candidate has served his or her time and can be considered for nomination. As Rush (1969:211) argues in the case of the Labour Party:

> the candidate is usually able to establish himself in a secure occupation which he can use as a stepping-stone to a political career, the initial stages of which can be embarked upon well before the age of thirty. *Active* service in the party is itself regarded as an adequate substitute for long service, while to *contest* several local elections will often satisfy demands for local government experience. [emphasis in original]

In the Conservative Party, it may also be the case that 'local government experience is regarded as a partial substitute for the social background which these candidates lack ... (but) occasionally ... it is viewed as a limiting factor, as an indication of the applicant's parochial outlook and lack of wider experience' (Rush 1969:79).

Patterns of access for local political leaders have emerged as indirect — mediated through the associations — and rather weak, because local politicians and associations could not count on parliamentary support for their aspirations. This was shown quite clearly in the local government reform process in England and Wales, when determined pressure by local politicians was almost completely ignored by their national counterparts. However, the lack of direct access and weak support at a national level only became a problem for the local authorities when central government sought to impose controversial policy priorities. Apart from structural reorganization and issues such as the 1972 Housing Finance Act, this has not occurred very often in the postwar period.

All this describes briefly patterns of access between central and local government as they exist in England. It is worth noting that in Wales, Scotland and Northern Ireland a more informal and personalized network of relationships exists. In these parts of the country, a minister of cabinet rank, with his own office, is responsible for most local government functions. Local politicians know their parliamentary colleagues better, and vice versa; they often belong to the same network of social, economic and political organizations; and the occupation of different political offices is more common than in England. It is thus much easier for an individual authority to deal with the centre directly, as Keating et al. (1983) have suggested. However, the extent to which this results in policy outcomes different to those achieved in England seems open to debate; in areas seen from Whitehall as crucial to the metropolitan core, territorial offices have far less room for manoeuvre than in those seen as less important (Goldsmith, 1985, Rose 1982). Again, the dual polity description seems applicable, as it was in the case of regional offices, although the territorial ones have more extensive powers and greater discretion. They are expected to manage their peripheries, leaving the core free to deal with matters of high politics (Bulpitt, 1983).

The dual polity in the 1980s
Like the expansion of government generally, the process of growth in local services in the postwar period was not particularly controversial (Heclo, 1981). Central government appeared to continue the broad, high-discretion approach to local services, and, as in earlier periods, even to take cues for national policy from local practice and ideas. Some functions were indeed taken away from local government, but many rapidly expanding services, such as education and personal social services, remained. During the 1960s and early 1970s — period of postwar growth — local government professional networks in many policy communities became dominant influences over policy. In typically incremental fashion, new services and higher standards were grafted on to the local government system, all capable of being financed by increasing central grant — the product of a rising tax income that was one of the 'fiscal dividends' of economic growth (Rose and Peters, 1978). Public expenditure in general, and local government spending in particular, continued on an upward spiral, with the Treasury bemoaning its loss of control over ceilings (Pliatzky, 1980). By this time, central government departments were beginning to establish regional offices, to deal with the problems and claims of individual local authorities and thereby reduce the need for direct contact between the ministry and the authorities. The regions lacked any form of discretion that would have enabled them to establish the more direct relationships of complicity that can be found between local heads of field services and the prefect, on the one hand, and local *notables* on the other, in France. They were empowered to approve smaller capital expenditure projects and to recommend approval of larger ones to headquarters. Yet the

formulae for allocation, as well as the formal limitations on regional officials, meant that civil servants who sought to act outside their formal powers — who 'went native' and zealously pushed the claims of their region — would find themselves unable to claim extra resources, and special claims would go unheard. These regional offices further enabled the centre to keep the locality at arm's length, while the growing status of the associations meant that Whitehall was spared direct contact with individual local authorities and was increasingly able to deal with representatives of local government.

Because of fears of continued loss of control over expenditure, and because the spending departments themselves were moving towards the use of planning systems to help to shape the services for which they were responsible, the early 1970s saw a move towards a corporative and directive style of central relations with local authorities that did not immediately manifest itself in changes in the formal statutory relationship (Rhodes, 1986). The establishment of the Consultative Council on Local Government Finance, with the introduction of planning systems in areas such as town planning, housing and transport, meant that the centre had the detailed information, as well as the close relations with the national professional bodies and local authority associations, it needed if it was to impose its will on the localities. Both professional and local authority associations accepted the invitation to the spider's web with alacrity, believing their special relationship with the centre would increase their ability to influence central policy decisions. The onslaught of the financial crisis, with the subsequent threat to welfare state services, showed the opposite to be the case. As the centre, under Labour from 1976 and the Conservatives from 1979, sought to reduce government expenditure in general and local spending in particular, the representatives of the professional networks found that, by and large, they were unable to protect their interests. Rate capping, reductions in grant, the mandatory sale of council houses, and new grant systems with targets, clawbacks and other penalties, were all introduced under the new style of directive government headed by Mrs Thatcher.

Thus, from the centre's point of view, the nineteenth-century practice of distancing the locality from central concerns continues in the late 1980s. The commonly observed tendency for contacts between central and local government to be made at the level of permanent official cannot be purely a product of central government actors' dispositions (Lee, 1962; Griffith, 1966). Rhodes (1986), and Gyford and James (1983) report cases of local politicians who had little or no direct contact with central government, or even saw the need for it. Nevertheless, the nature of the conflicts that have occurred since the mid-1970s has had one effect on the channels of access between centre and locality. As Gyford and James (1983) illustrate, it has opened and expanded the partisan link, with both major parties (and to a lesser extent the minor ones) giving more attention to local government matters and developing links between local politicians and their parliamentary counterparts. There is much greater co-ordination between different authorities, their politicians, party groups on the national local government associations and the parliamentary parties than was the case ten years ago. The conflict also saw the arrival of local Labour politicians who have begun to achieve national status and prominence, for example Kenneth Livingstone of the Greater London Council and David Blunkett of Sheffield City Council. Many Conservative politicians have been critical of the way in which the government's policies towards metropolitan reorganization and local expenditure have allowed these leaders to attract substantial publicity and public sympathy.

These changes, primarily affecting the Labour Party, in conjunction with the rate-capping legislation have opened up the possibility of further shifts in patterns of access — the expansion of channels of direct access to the centre through a strategy of non-co-operation and direct obstruction. In early 1984, for example, Liverpool City Council dealt directly with the Department of the Environment and the Secretary of State over its expenditure target and level of grant support. By threatening disruption, through passing an illegal budget in which income failed to balance expenditure, the council won modest concessions; additional grant aid as well as a public relations victory. So strong was the government's initial resolve to stand firm that the eventual compromise appeared to both Labour and Conservative supporters as a victory; so much so that the Secretary of State for the Environment felt moved to challenge this impression in the letters column of *The Times*. What this case specifically revealed was the great difficulty experienced by the centre in dealing with detailed problems posed by one recalcitrant authority, albeit one with some of the worst sets of economic and social problems in the country. If this kind of defiance to the application of rate-capping legislation is repeated consistently in future years, the implications for central –local relations will be immense. The centre will find that it has to deal directly with a number of awkward local authorities on an individual basis, and, far from distancing itself from the localities, will find itself heavily involved in their work. This would perhaps mark the most significant development to date in central –local relations, since detailed intervention would not only run counter to the principle of high local discretion — one of the pillars of the dual polity — but, because of the nature of direct relationships and the prominence accorded to local issues in national policy-making forums, might eventually bridge the political gulf between the two arms of government. In practice, however, the centre has managed to avoid such entanglements to date.

Conclusions

What appears to have been admired as the basis for local self-government in Britain was a dual polity tradition. While other countries, such as Germany and France — possibly following the experience of absolutism — developed a system of territorial government consistent, at least in theory, with the unified hierarchy of the *Obrigkeitsstaat*, in Britain formal legal discretion was granted in the delivery of a wide range of local services. That the twentieth century appears to have brought greater homogeneity in service provision (compare, for example, Webb, 1911, with Newton and Sharpe, 1984) cannot be attributed solely to national legislation or financial incentives, although these have clearly increased over the past eighty-six years. Of course, a large number of national factors of a non-statutory nature have also shaped service development; above all, a variety of authors — perhaps beginning with Finer (1950) and his notion of 'enforced collaboration', and running through to Dunleavy's (1981a) discussion of 'ideological corporatism' — has emphasized the importance of the nationally shared values of local officials in limiting the variation in the standards and policies of individual local authorities. Of course, in practice there are a variety of constraints on local authority discretion. But the crucial point is that these have not been exclusively statutory; the existing statutory obligations in principle leave much room for the exercise of local discretion.

Yet it is precisely this aspect of the dual polity — the broad allocation of a large number of functions to local government — that undermined the foundations on which political influence appears to be (at least partly) based in countries such as Italy, France and the United States; the ability to use one's position as the elected representative of a locality to influence national political and bureaucratic actors. The dual polity allowed local politicians to exercise direct influence over local issues without continual recourse to direct contact with their national counterparts. The development of national associations of local authorities helped to ensure that, on the occasions when central government wanted to enter some form of dialogue with local government, there was no need to take up direct contacts. The professional associations and the expertise found among local bureaucracies obviated the need to use centralized technical expertise to develop local policies.

The experiences of the late 1970s on have shown the importance of the three broad bases of the dual polity; the extensive functions and discretion of local government, and the separation of national from local politics, with the latter subordinate to the former. It is the political weakness of local government that has made it relatively easy for central government to erode the other two bases of the dual polity.

6
France

Yves Mény

Introduction: centralization and decentralization

France is frequently considered the prototype of centralization, with its ideal-typical demographic, economic, administrative and political concentration of resources in Paris. Yet a more detailed analysis reveals that such generalizations are an over-statement, even if they are not completely wrong. France has more local authorities than any other West European country — four times more than Germany and Italy, for example; in addition it has proved the most resistant to changes in its local government system, and the French political system is permeated by the influence of local values, right to the core of the central government.

The ambiguity of the French system explains why some analyses using a particular time frame or perspective, tend to emphasize its decentralized nature, while others, using different periods and perspectives, underline its centralization (Ashford, 1982). Another factor which helps to explain the divergence of these points of view is related to the nature of local government research. For a long time, studies of centralization and decentralization were monopolized by lawyers, who naturally tended to emphasize the hierarchy of norms — the inferiority and dependence of the local authorities, and central government's strength of control and powers of tutelage. It was only in the 1960s that the dominant perception of a highly centralized system was modified under the influence of French sociologists (Groupe de Sociologie des Organisations, headed by Michel Crozier) and British and American political scientists, who were concerned less with the formal rules of the system and more with its informal operation, and with the compromise and evasion that gave local actors substantial room for manoeuvre (Crozier et al., 1974: Kesselman, 1967).

To a certain extent, this involved the rediscovery of a line of thought opened by Alexis de Tocqueville in *L'Ancien Regime and the Revolution*, when he asserted that 'the rules are rigid but the practice is limp'.

Nevertheless, the differences in perception cannot be attributed solely to methodological disputes or conflicts. The 'local government revisited' of the 1970s and 1980s differs substantially from that of the immediate postwar period, even if certain fundamental structural traits persist. What are the unchanging characteristics of centralization and decentralization since the end of the Second World War, and what are the transient ones?

The period since 1945 has been marked by three stages of profound political, social and economic changes: the immediate postwar years, the late 1950s and early 1960s, and the years since 1968. The first brought both radical changes and the reaffirmation of traditional values. For both private citizen and local authority, the changes were linked with the nationalization programme and the creation of a social security system. The nationalizations, in particular gas and electricity, were the most marked example of the tendency towards centralization, in some form or another, of public services for which ultimate responsibility previously lay with the municipalities or *départements*. Social security constituted another homogenizing factor, because it assured a redistribution of resources independent of territorial location. Politically, the constitution of 1946 sought to strengthen local authorities by limiting the role of the prefect solely to that of the representative of the state, by granting special legal status to large towns and declining to set up a regional level of government. In any case, the failure to implement these reforms meant that the legal and political order of the Third Republic was maintained more or less intact.

The end of the Fourth Republic and beginning of the Fifth not only brought institutional reform; it also meant a process of economic and social transformation never before seen in France. The country experienced an urban revolution at last, which highlighted the inadequacy of housing, public services and infrastructure for coping with the influx of rural migrants, and underlined the inability of local structures to cope with the new tasks they had to take on.

This crisis was to have profound political implications, although the Gaullists preferred to approach it through a series of vague reforms. In fact, the leftist opposition, which had fallen back to its position within local government, saw the defeat of the Gaullist reform proposals as a last line of defence against complete exclusion from the political system. Local government thus became the arena for much wider conflicts between the Gaullists and a curious coalition of centre, left and extreme right-wing *notables*. Gradually, the status quo became identified with 'democracy' and 'liberty', even though it caused severe problems in terms of service delivery (Mény, 1974). Meanwhile, in trying to bypass local notables — of left or right — by relying on *forces vives*, Gaullism succeeded in strengthening the regional level. Yet, for the most part, Gaullist governments had to be content with marginal adjustments to the status quo, such as the creation of ad hoc authorities providing services across local government boundaries, rather than the more radical reforms they would have liked to implement.

The years between the late 1960s and the early 1980s mark a third period, characterized by a reduction in centre—periphery conflicts and the creation of a near-universal consensus about the reforms that should and should not be introduced. Politicians of all major parties abandoned the idea of territorial reform and turned to the regional level of government. For their part, local elites were happy with fiscal reforms that guaranteed them an adequate resource base, yet appeared to deepen divisions between the large towns, which were becoming progressively more autonomous, and the thousands of small municipalities dependent on départements and the central state.

Finally, in 1981, for the first time since 1958, the same coalition that dominated the periphery also held power at the centre. This, with the consensus on the desirability of reform, allowed the left to achieve what has been emphatically labelled '*la grande affaire du septennat*'.

Taken together, the postwar years have been characterized by a diversification of local authorities and of the functions they carry out. More than ever before, the urban—rural cleavage represents the fundamental division in French politics. The urban areas were forced to take complete or partial responsibility for functions that could not be guaranteed by the state. Local authorities became the largest source of public-sector investment and had to manage the services they created. Functions that did not exist twenty years ago, such as cultural programmes, now make up more than 10 per cent of the budgets of most large towns. The relationship between central and local government has also been modified — the notables have declined in power as the role of parties has increased — but its role has not fundamentally changed. More than ever, the osmosis between central and local political power continues, showing itself in a variety of forms; the 'nationalization' of local elections; the expansion of *cumul des mandats*; greater localism in national politics; above all through the relationship with the Senate, and the circulation of elites between national and local public service.

One of the main changes concerns the local authorities' autonomy in relation to the central state. It is always difficult to measure the degree to which local authorities are autonomous, because the dimensions that can be used are so numerous and the contexts in which it can be assessed so diverse. There is, however, one reliable indicator: the presence or absence of protests from local political leaders. These vigorously opposed the ascendancy of the centre in the 1960s, but rarely complain today. One does not have to look to the recent reform of the *Loi Deferre*, which substituted juridical a posteriori controls for the a priori tutelage of the prefect, for an explanation. On the contrary, the reform acknowledges the centre's inability to exercise its traditional controls, whether because of political resistance, in particular from the large towns, or bureaucratic pressures, such as overload problems.

The main reasons for the absence of widespread discontent among local political leaders was the improvement in local finances that derived from central transfers in the form of unconditional 'global grants', allowing local authorities to meet their obligations. This development was positive in terms of local service provision, and also enhanced local autonomy and the authorities' ability to influence central policy making. It underlines the fundamental role of local authorities in France, and is worth examining more closely.

The political importance of the local system

Between 1870 and 1981, France's local government system was organized on the basis of laws passed in conformity with the wishes of republicans, in reaction to the empire of Napoleon III, and conservatives and ruralists, as a means of opposing revolutionary movements and the Paris Commune.

The law of 1871 for the départements and of 1884 for the *communes* imposed a common legal framework on all local authorities, be they industrial or rural departements, large towns or small villages. The framework was designed for rural settings and totally inadequate for metropolitan areas. Only the City of Paris avoided being put in such a straitjacket, but only by finding itself once again under direct state tutelage. The best illustration of the distrust of large towns that this reflected is the decision to 'freeze' the boundaries of local communes, which remain inviolable despite the economic and demographic transformation of the country.

This cumbersome system continued only because of the relative economic decline of the interwar period and because of the pressure of more urgent problems after 1945 — the Cold War, de-colonization and regional underdevelopment. While it appeared necessary to reform the local system, and the Gaullists were the first to make a serious effort in this direction, local politico-administrative structures in France were so well entrenched that it was almost impossible to transform them in the radical directions taken in Britain and the Scandinavian countries. Since it was impossible to reconstruct the local system from a *tabula rasa*, the government had to come to terms with it, despite its archaic structure, in order to allow for the provision of public services. This model of obstruction and adaptation shows the importance of local authorities from two points of view: the political and the financial.

The political importance of local government derives from a combination of many factors. Most important, if not explicitly acknowledged, is that the rural community dominating local government served as a means to counter the plans, often regarded as 'dangerous', of left-wing parties that were stronger in urban areas.

The influence of the rural community is above all quantitative — 90 per cent of France's 36,494 communes have fewer than 2000 inhabitants and only 885 — or 2 per cent — have more than 10,000. This explains why almost 40 per cent of mayors come from peasant backgrounds, although the agricultural sector accounts for only 7 per cent of the economically active population.

Likewise, the departements are still dominated by representatives of rural cantons, despite attempts to provide fairer representation for urban areas. The combination of this over-representation and the shift to the right in mass attitudes gave the right an overwhelming preponderance in the departements: the 1985 cantonal elections gave the opposition control of sixty-nine of the ninety-five *conseils généraux*. Elsewhere, local rural influence is exaggerated, even in central state institutions, for example the Senate, which is elected indirectly by the local authorities among whom rural representatives predominate. One can understand the irritation of the left under the Third Republic with a conservative assembly — dubbed the 'chamber of agriculture' — which in effect had a right of veto on all government reform proposals. One can understand even more readily if it's remembered that the only two referendums in French history to have returned a negative majority concerned the abolition or radical transformation of the Senate.

Again, the Gaullists' caution, as far as local government reform was concerned, can be partly explained by the dependence of central government on local notables: it was to avoid a presidential election by parliamentary representatives. Owing to his inability to secure the direct election of the President, de Gaulle imposed election of the President by a college of around 80,000 *grands électeurs* in which once again local politicians were over-represented. Georges Vedel commented, with irony, that the president was elected by the 'rye and the chestnut'. The constitutional reform of 1962, which introduced direct election of the president, was designed precisely to prevent de Gaulle's successors becoming prisoners of the notables. Finally, the intertwining of the local and the central has been strengthened by the expansion in *cumul des mandats*, which will be examined in greater detail below.

Unable to change the system radically, successive French governments were constrained in the way in which they could come to terms with local government. Like the fox in Aesop's fable of the sour grapes, since the 1970s they have rejoiced in the democratic treasure of nearly 500,000 elected councillors. This demanded the introduction of complex procedures, institutions of co-operation between the localities and revisions to the local financial system in order to square the circle by distributing adequate and more or less uniform sums of money over a territory divided into ninety-five departements and 36,000 communes (Ashford, 1982).

This tinkering with the financial side allowed the basic structure — a rural-centred system covering all local authorities — to continue. The reforms of 1981–83 showed that some lessons had been learned from earlier efforts, but still constituted a mirror image of those of 1871 and 1884: they were designed as uniform and general, and applied to all local authorities. Yet behind this facade of uniformity, it is clear that they were conceived by and for the *grands notables* of the towns and departements. Small communes and departements with low populations do not change very much: they were unable to, despite the new legal framework.

In effect, the new autonomy given to elected officials, the removal of the old system of prefectoral tutelage and the transfer of functions are instruments that can only be used effectively when adequate political and financial resources are available. The Loi Defferre changes nothing for the overwhelming majority of communes, which lack the means to make it work. On the other hand, the mayors of large towns and the most active of the departements' 'bosses' have managed to regularize and widen the scope for autonomy they had managed to create for themselves by acting at the margins of, or even against, the law.

Functional allocation and discretion

The distribution of functions between the state and the local authorities, and among regions, departements and communes, follows neither logic nor strict rules. The precise nature of this distribution results from various factors. First, it derives from an historical and ideological legacy. In the nineteenth century the liberals, on the one hand, and the monarchists, on the other, defended local liberties on the grounds that local affairs should be dealt with at the most appropriate level, in particular the commune.

This analysis aimed to keep centralization and the power of the administration in check, in particular under the Second Empire, and found its clearest expression in the Nancy Manifesto of 1867: 'national matters go to the state, regional to the regions and local to the commune.' The laws of 1871 and 1884 were the perfect juridical translation of this principle: 'The *conseil général* rules by its deliberations the matters of the départements; the *conseil municipal* rules by its deliberations the matters of the commune.' Given the minimal role of the public sector, the imprecise definition of these terms did not appear to pose any problems at the time. A few years later, the concept of 'local matters' was clarified as a result of conflicts between left and right: economic and social intervention ('municipal socialism') was to be limited or not undertaken at all, and the definition of local matters was to exclude the former altogether — in principle at least, although the exceptions were to go on increasing in number. In other words, departements and communes had, in the traditional liberal conception, a general competence over affairs in their territory, except for matters considered private, such as the freedom of commerce and industry.

The second factor affecting the distribution of functions was the need to lay down general principles and to guarantee that the local authorities would carry out their tasks. This explains why the general law (Code) of the communes made the distinction between discretionary functions (*compétences facultatives*) and mandatory functions (*compétences obigatoires*); the latter were enforced by the prefect, even if this meant additional spending. Otherwise, services have been localized or nationalized according to the priorities of the centre. These variations highlight the artificial nature of the concept of local matters in France.

The third factor results from the expansion of the welfare state, from urban development and from the need to reconcile the provision of essential public services on an egalitarian basis with the multiplicity of actors charged with providing them. The centre was obliged to increase its intervention in order to guarantee this homogenization at the very time that the local authorities were given a share of the state's own functional tasks in an effort to alleviate the financial burden imposed by increased intervention. For example, the centre subsidized the construction of primary schools (a local government function) yet asked for the authorities to contribute to the costs of university construction and the extension of the telephone network. By the end of the 1970s, the distribution of functions no longer corresponded to any form of logic and better resembled a dense jungle than an ordered division of tasks.

It is therefore impossible to state what precisely are 'local government tasks'. The main mandatory functions of local government are school building, police, fire, public health, land use planning, road maintenance and some social transfer payments. Yet even here not all communes carry out mandatory tasks, either because central state provision of the service, for example police, is sufficient, or because the commune is simply too small to sustain it. Moreover, the allocation of tasks in France varies substantially from that of Britain and the Scandinavian countries: instead of being responsible for the delivery of a particular service, for example education, local government is charged, in many policy areas, only with relatively narrowly defined components of the service, such as school buildings and teachers' housing. The major discretionary functions are culture

and tourism, social assistance and aid to industry. Such is the
variability of local government tasks that Kobielski (1974) uses
regression analysis to predict what functions local authorities will
carry out, in the same way that political scientists in Britain and
America used it to predict levels of spending on various services.
Figures for total expenditure are given for *collectivités locales*, that
is, including departements and regions, in Table 1. Collectivités
locales are responsible for 20.5 per cent of current public spending.
Since the current budgets of the departements formed 31 per cent of
collectivite locale spending in 1981, the communes were responsible
for around 14 per cent of current expenditure. More substantial is the
collectivites locales' contribution to capital expenditure — 74.5 per
cent; on the basis of the same calculations as used for current
spending, the contribution of the communes alone is a large one,
accounting for 61 per cent of total capital expenditure.
    Table 1 shows that local authorities have a minor role in providing
current expenditure for most public services, with two exceptions:

TABLE 1
France: distribution of public spending by function and level of
administration, 1981 (FF million)

		Consumption				Investment		
	Total	% central	% local	% social security	Total	% central	% local	% social security
Education	96,201	86.5	13.5	—	9970	26.9	73.1	—
Culture	6961	37.9	62.1	—	4337	14.2	85.8	—
Health	7824	12.0	15.0	73.0	726	9.0	51.6	39.4
Social services	19,643	11.7	23.0	65.3	1857	7.2	45.5	47.3
Housing/ urban dev.	13,672	15.8	84.2	—	22,093	12.9	87.1	—
Economic aid	14,181	80.5	19.5	—	2284	—	—	—
Gen. admin.	29,363	54.9	45.1	—	3873	20.3	79.7	—
Research	3649	100.0	—	—	795	100.0	—	—
Justice/ police	15,195	82.8	17.2	—	1225	39.5	60.5	—
Foreign affairs	2379	100.0	—	—	149	100.0	—	—
Defence	58,019	100.0	—	—	1227	100.0	—	—
Transport	6375	60.5	39.5	—	9570	44.6	55.4	—
Other	3649	70.7	29.3		507	0.8	99.2	—
Total	277,111	72.8	20.8	6.7	58,663	33.5	74.5	2.0

Source: INSEE, *Données sociales*, Paris: INSEE, 1981.

culture, in which they account for 62 per cent of total spending, and housing and urban development, in which they account for 84 per cent. The local authority contribution to housing expenditure is channelled largely through the HLMs (*Habitation à loyer moderé*), which are best considered as 'off-line' agencies of local government with a distinct system of funding and a relationship of tutelage with the departements (Duclaud-Williams, 1978). The relatively minor role of local authorities in current expenditure contrasts strongly with their role in all sectors of capital spending except research, foreign affairs and defence.

The reforms of 1981−83 could have radically reformed local government functions by reordering them and clarifying their modes of finance, so that each level of government had more clearly defined — and more — areas of autonomy. Indeed, an attempt was made to do this, but it remained limited by the absence of a reform of territorial structures and by the political necessity of operating according to general and uniform criteria. Neverthless, several important changes were introduced, although all their consequences cannot yet be assessed.

First, article 1 of Law No. 83−8, of 7 January 1983, modified the framework set out in the laws of 1871 and 1884 by stating that the communes, departements and regions 'govern by their deliberations the matters within their competence.' In other words, their field of intervention is no longer general, but varies according to the law that is attributed to each.

Second, the government sought to clarify the distribution of functions between the four territorial levels (state, region, departement, commune). It did this by resuming control over spending that had (contrary to the law) become decentralized, as in the field of justice and the police, by transferring functions shared by central and local authorities entirely to the local level, and by concentrating major responsibility for certain tasks (*specialisation*) among particular types of authority; examples include economic development in the regions, social affairs in the departement and land-use planning in the communes. Nevertheless, in spite of these good intentions, the allocation of functions remains extremely complex. To use a well-worn American analogy, the reformers sought to create a distribution of functions resembling a layer cake, with distinct differences between each level, yet the system ended up as a marble cake, in which the distinctions are never clear or even. In housing, planning and education, for example, the distribution of tasks remains confused and at best threatens to be a source of bureaucratic complexity and at worst to generate conflicts between different levels of government. Although the government did indeed seek to clarify the position, and abolished all forms of tutelage by one level of government over another, a reading of the legal documents and observation of the progress of their implementation gives the impression that the reform is more by way of an imperfect patch-up than a fundamental recasting of the system.

The reforms of 1981–83 have also given rise to discussion through the fact that tutelage has been abolished. Before the dimensions of this change are examined, let us remember that there were three types of formal or informal tutelage; administrative tutelage, exercised by the prefect, over the decisions of local authorities; financial tutelage, exercised in principle by the prefect, but, de facto, by the Finance Ministry; and technical tutelage, of various sorts, which imposed model norms or actions prepared within central ministries.

Of these three forms of tutelage, the first was questionably the most acceptable, in particular to the small communes which regarded the prefecture as more of a source of help and advice than an organ of surveillance. It is significant that, according to a survey conducted by the *Association des Maires de France*, in 4873 communes spread across sixty-three departements, only 35 per cent of mayors believed the operation of the new legislative measures would give them greater freedom to their commune. Moreover, as one would guess, this is more likely to be the view the larger the commune, thus confirming the hypothesis that the reforms are more likely to affect large communes than small. The extent of the reform is rather more limited than is suggested by the way in which it is presented in public debates: first, because the number of local decisions annulled under the old system was small — at most several dozen a year for each departement. Second, because the reform transforms the structure of control less than it appears to. Before the reform, local decisions had to be passed to the prefect and were considered valid as long as the prefect did not annul them within a statutorily defined time limit. From now on, the prefect, having been informed of all local authority decisions, has to transmit all requests for annulment to the regional administrative tribunal within fifteen days. In this two-week period, the prefect can not only threaten the local authority with legal action, but can also seek to persuade it to modify its contentious decision. Figures for April 1983 to March 1984 can be used to show the reform's limitations in this respect: 2.3 million decisions were referred to prefectures, 992 became the object of legal appeal by the *Commissaires de la République*, but of these 418 — almost half — were withdrawn in the process of appeal. This points to the continuance of the informal discussions that took place in the past between the representatives of the government and of local authorities. It should nevertheless be emphasized that, from the standpoint of legal guarantees, intervention by a third party, in this case a judge, is in principle a better solution than that of the earlier prefectoral tutelage. Even if the commissaires had won their appeals in 80 per cent of cases, 20 per cent (which could have been simply annulled, according to the old system of tutelage) would still be recognized as valid by the administrative tribunals.

The second form of tutelage — financial— is a source of profound irritation to elected politicians, who protest against the — in their eyes excessive — intervention by the Ministry of Finance and occasionally the prefect. Without abolishing the powers of the Commissaire de la République completely, the law makes a major change by substituting a posteriori controls, exercised by the regional accounting authorities (*chambres régionales des comptes*, which are to be helped in their massive job of financial scrutiny by sections of the Finance Ministry that also handle local budgets), for the old a priori measures. Nevertheless, the commissaire keeps, for example, the power to write spending on obligatory functions into local budgets. The main result of this reform is likely to be the reinforcement of controls based on legal measures at the expense of those based on pragmatism; the strengthening of juridical measures at the expense of informal negotiations.

The third form of tutelage is both the most diffuse and the most difficult to eliminate. In a primarily symbolic measure, the law of 2 March 1982 determined that technical forms of tutelage could only result from an enabling law or decree, and that the elaboration of a general code of norms would come within two years (put back by two years in 1983). Despite these good intentions, it has proved difficult to remove existing forms of technical tutelage and even more so to prevent them from re-emerging in new forms. For example, the practice of forming contracts between the centre and local government, which in principle respects the wishes of both parties, may turn out to be an insidious form of interference by the centre which, through the subsidies it offers and negotiates, can succeed in determining the policies of local authorities that are both beneficiaries and dependents. Such has been the growth of these contracts that the Minister of the Interior, Gaston Deferre, was himself alarmed about this new 'soft' strategy of the central ministries.

Even if the reforms of 1981–83 do not address all the problems, they do constitute a positive development for local authorities which, through the pressures they have placed on the governments of the Fifth Republic, have been able to increase their functions, their room for manoeuvre and their resources. The local authorities' strength can be measured by the improvement in their financial position over the past twenty years. In the mid-1960s they were in a dire position, and the state had the means to exert extraordinarily strong pressure on them by virtue of being their only source of new resources, through transfers or new taxes; today, the authorities have succeeded in completely reversing the position. The departements and regions have four taxes at their disposal: on buildings, land, dwellings and businesses. The authorities can fix the rate at which these taxes are levied, but the increase or decrease in any one is linked with that of the others, to prevent any single tax being raised or lowered too sharply. The most important, and contentious, of these taxes is the business tax (*taxe professionnelle*), which makes up about one-half of total receipts. Nevertheless, local taxes as a whole make up only 50 per cent of the resources of the departements and communes. The rest is made up of borrowing and, above all, central state grants. These are mainly block grants, not tied to specific services, which the local authorities are free to use as they choose. The most important is the *dotation globale de fonctionnement* (DGF), which gives the authorities a flexible resource calculated as a percentage of valued-added tax (VAT) receipts. The DGF amounted to FF 66,000 million in 1985. The *dotation globale d'équipement* (DGE) set up in 1982 was designed progressively to change the specific grants for capital purposes in block allocations to be spent by the authorities as they please. DGE amounted to only FF 2,500 million in 1985.

The *dotation globale de décentralisation*, which reached FF 13,000 million, serves to compensate authorities for the new functions given to them since 1982. In total, the authorities in 1985 received FF 128,000 million, nearly all of it free of conditions. This is remarkable, since the transfers from the centre are large and can be used as the authorities wish; the resources transferred are growing more rapidly than those available to the centre and are rising above the level of inflation; local levies are also growing rapidly, so that central state taxes (but not social insurance contributions) are declining in relative terms.

The financial situation of the local authorities, varying as it does from one region to another, remains on the whole very favourable, above all by comparison with the 1960s or with their counterparts in most other western countries.

Access

Centre–periphery studies convey an impression of two separate, hierarchically distinct entities, with the periphery generally subordinate to the values, norms and decisions of the centre. French experience suggests a somewhat different interpretation, because it is characterized more by osmosis than separation. In addition, the interpenetration between centre and periphery is linked with constant exchanges and overlap between the administrative and political sphere. Thus the question is less one of access, of which there is plenty, but of specific modes of access.

As is well known, one basic characteristic of center—periphery relations in France is the cumul des mandats. More than 75 per cent of deputies and 90 per cent of senators are also mayors or members of municipal, general and/or regional councils. This tradition has persisted since the Third republic, was strengthened further in the Fifth and reached its apotheosis with the Socialist victory in 1981. In fact, the left had patiently to reconquer the communes, departements and regions before translating (and thereby realizing the benefits of) the long march through the local institutions into national success in the 'divine surprise' of 1981. The Fifth Republic helped to accentuate the cumul phenomenon in several ways: at first by instituting the single-member majority voting system which, given the weakness of party organization in France, provided a *député* with a firm anchorage in his or her constituency.

Second, the extension of bipartisanship throughout the political system has led the notables to develop closer links with national parties and for the parties to seek out local points of pressure; eventually, at least for the Gaullists, the traditional career path of politicians went into reverse — having gained power at the centre, they sought to reinforce their position at the periphery. This led to a concentration of political resources in the hands of a small number, and made some positions unassailable. The defeat in 1985 of the Deputy Mayor of Grenoble, first elected twenty years earlier, or the persistent challenge to Defferre, who ran Marseille from the end of the Second World War to 1986, are only exceptions to the rule. The phenomenon of the notable has remained, even though the parties have become stronger over the past twenty years.

It is the notable who controls the party locally rather than the other way round. This may perhaps be reversed as a result of changes in electoral systems: in communes with populations of less than 3500, election by majority on second ballot, in communes with populations of more than 3500, election by majority on second ballot, modified by minority proportional representation of opposition parties. In the departements, election is by single-member majority on second ballot, using cantons as electoral districts; in the regions, there is proportional representation using departements as electoral districts, as in polls for the National Assembly; and for presidential elections, majority on second ballot. For the European elections, proportional representation is based on a single, national electoral district.

The reforms bring two important changes. First, they introduce the principle of direct election by universal suffrage at every level, including the region from 1986, making it more difficult to accumulate functions and mandates at the four lowest levels. Second, by introducing proportionality at the regional and national level, the changes reduce the bipolarity and personalization that have characterized electoral contests to date. At these two levels, the parties will again acquire a dominant position in drawing up lists of candidates. These changes may have various results: reinforcement of national controls over deputies, and enlargement of political elites, as parties are forced to distribute offices rather than hand them to individual politicians.

In addition, a law adopted in December 1985 puts limits on the cumul des mandats. Since the general election of March 1986 politicians are allowed to hold only two offices; however, the rule disregards mandates in cities of fewer than 20,000 inhabitants. This new set of regulations could produce some changes: the creation of specific regional elites, or the colonization of regional assemblies by the départements' *conseillers généraux* or by defeated deputies. The reforms will alter not only the national political scene, but also the relationship between centre and periphery, by strengthening the role of the parties to the detriment of that of the notables — for whom the natural refuge will be the Senate — and by creating competing elites at the local level (especially at département and regional level).

However, many politicians will retain two mandates (and mayors of small communes possibly three), making the management of their constituencies difficult for them. The decentralizing reforms of 1981−83 have highlighted this difficulty in particular, as well as the shallowness of the appealing facade the administration and politicians have set up: the new regional presidents — mainly deputies and senators — find themselves charged with responsibilities previously carried out by the prefect, without having the necessary time or preparation to fulfil them.

For their part, many prefects, subprefects and directors of state field services feared a decline in their responsibilities and backed both decentralization and the change in government. Many were closely tied to the old majority parties and preferred the challenge of a prominent post in local government to a middle-ranking post at the centre. They sometimes became cabinet director for the local leader or director of local services, putting their experience at the disposal of the elected representative and exercising, de facto, administrative power. The weeks after the reforms saw a remarkably swift adaptation to them on the part of political and administrative elites. To take away the prefect's role as executive agent of the regions and départements was to risk breaking the close links between administrators and politicians, of whom the prefect was frequently the co-ordinator and prime mover. Today, it appears that the functional duality found under the old prefectoral system has been replaced by an organic duality still controlled by the agents of central government: on the one hand, the *Commissaire de la République* (as representative of the state), and on the 'other', the close adviser to the elected representative (usually a prefect or other central state official, on secondment).

These new mechanisms, set up in 1982–83 without the government intervening even to limit the temporary exodus of top civil servants, could only be reinforced by the reform of local government service in 1983. The changes can be summarized in a single sentence: the local service was brought into line with the national civil service. Curiously, this reform, which has brought about a 'nationalization' of the local government service, has been presented as a decentralizing measure, and this has never been challenged. The paradox can be understood only in terms of the French bureaucracy's abiding conviction that every civil servant should have a *statut* (that is, a set of rules organizing his or her rights and duties), and that the statut be national to be worthy of such a name. The harmonization of the two statuts is in particular designed to allow mobility between national and local public service. In the short term, this nationalization will facilitate the transfer of personnel resulting from the shift of functions — in fact, it would be impossible without such homogenization. In the medium to long term, the reform must strengthen the interchange of personnel, at least at the higher levels, between national and local public service (the central administration, through budgetary control, refuses to allow the creation of posts that demand highly qualified officials), the interchange being solely to the benefit of the central administrators, graduates of the Ecole Nationale d'Administration (ENA). For ENA graduates, *détachement* offers not only wider opportunities — and often better pay — than a post within the central administration (which will become increasingly hard to find because of the rising number of students at ENA), but also provides an escape route for some when the national government changes. The more the local system offers a means of rescue for civil servants removed from positions of political responsibility at the national level, the more opportunity there will be to expand the spoils system.

The periphery possesses other powerful means of influencing central policies, in particular through associations of elected representatives. Each party has sought to organize its own representatives and to attract those who vaguely sympathize without actually being party members, so there are several such organizations. However, their influence on the development of national policy is weak, thanks to the party political divisions and the fact that their main purpose is to screen the weakness of party organization in the localities. On the other hand, associations organized on a corporatist rather than a political basis are very powerful. Most important is the *Association des Maires de France*, which embraces nearly all communes countrywide; next comes the permanent assembly of *Presidents des Conseils Généraux*, which speaks for departmental executives of all political colours, and finally there are the two associations of *Presidents des Conseils Régionaux*, representing the majority parties and the opposition, each in about one-half of the regions. Links between the two associations are not entirely lacking, and it is generally agreed that this represents one of the rare examples of dialogue between the elected representatives of the opposing parties. These associations are powerful primarily because of their influence through the Senate (the president of the Association des Maires de France is usually a powerful member of the Senate); the government could not contemplate local reform without their express or tacit support. One of the authors of the Loi Defferre confided in private that the measures had been derived in part from those put forward by the government of President Giscard d'Estaing in 1980–81, as amended by the Senate. This is a good example of the continuity and pragmatism that typify the French system.

Nevertheless, the Association des Maires de France is the victim of its own ecumenicalism: because of the structure of local government in France, the small communes, which are not really interested in the problems of the larger towns, have a large majority. In response, the towns set up a 'study group' of mayors, although they maintained their membership of the association. The study group constitutes a specific pressure group, small in numbers but representing the majority of the population and dealing with the most important problems facing urban areas. For example, all local finance reforms must meet the requirements of small communes as well as large towns. Thus, the DGF paid to the local authorities by the centre (and making up around 25 per cent of their income) comprises three elements: *dotation forfaitaire, dotation de péréquation* and *concours particuliers*, with the latter primarily intended for communes with fewer than 2000 inhabitants and a weak resource base, as well as for conurbations. In this way, small and large communes alike are kept happy.

Nonetheless, despite their strong influence, plus their ability to represent all departements or communes, these pressure groups are weakened by their heterogeneity. Elected representatives within these associations are united when it comes to resisting central encroachment or extracting subsidies from the centre, but more divided with respect to various other government initiatives. Cleavages based on party lines, ideology and interests prevent the associations from presenting a common front. The best example of this is the progressive introduction of a regional level of government, despite little enthusiasm on the part of local elected representatives.

The regional dimension

The creation of regions in France provides the best possible example of an incremental process. Between 1955 (the year the *Comités de Développement Economique* were set up) and 1986 (when the first elections by universal suffrage to the Conseils Régionaux took place), a profound change has taken place which shows how wrong those pessimistic analyses were that doubted whether full regions would ever be established. The reasons for this are manifold and result from a convergence of interest among diverse, not to say conflicting, groups: beside regional traditionalists and those newly converted to socialism were Gaullist technocrats, Giscardiens and the majority of Christian-democratic centrists. This unlikely coalition was never strong enough to carry the reforms as far as the regionalists wanted, but did manage to ensure progressive development, or regionalism step by step. In the initial phases, the main element was the need to enlarge limited bases of electoral support; the main target of the strategy was the regional loyalists, who were mostly outside the major parties in the 1960s. After the Algerian War of 1962, for example, de Gaulle sought to eliminate the old notables, who had become increasingly hostile to him, by relying on *forces vives*, which he integrated with the committees of regional economic development (CODER). A fresh attempt in 1969 failed, but more for general political reasons than hostility towards regionalization. In opposition, the Socialist Party pursued the same campaign of wooing marginal groups whose support was needed for electoral victory. Thus the Socialists promised more than the Pompidou reforms, which they condemned as minimalist and ludicrous; even so, they were deeply divided over the issue, with new regionalists coming into conflict with the large number of Jacobins within the party.

Nevertheless, in practice Socialist leaders exploited the potential of the Pompidou reforms, even to the extent of going beyond what they envisaged. Despite the constraints of the omnipresent prefects, the absence of an elected regional assembly and limited resources, the most active presidents of regional councils were to turn the regional institution to their advantage. For example, the regional agencies could not hire personnel or finance current spending, they could only subsidize the capital spending of other public agencies (central state, departmental and local). Although devised as a framework to keep the regions in check, this power, skilfully used, became a useful means of shaping policy. At a time of scarce resources, the types of offer the regions made to other public organizations, such as a 30 to 40 per cent subvention for a capital project, were extremely attractive. The regions thus used to their own advantage one of the techniques the centre had long used to control them. The reforms of 1982–83 completed this evolution, hardly altering the structures already in place, but giving them the legitimacy conferred by universal suffrage. These reforms are characterized by the substitution of the elected representative for the prefect who, under the title Commissaire de la République, remains only the representative of the state; the election by universal suffrage of the Conseil Régional on the basis of proportional representation, and the expansion of functions (planning, economic intervention, professional training, and additional resources), to be further increased in 1986, when the limit on revenue-raising was lifted.

Regional resources (FF 15,000 million for the whole country, excluding Paris) and personnel (roughly 2500 employees) may be modest in relation to other types of subnational government organization, but the impact of the regions is important. In effect, the small size of their current operating and personnel costs allows them to invest 65 per cent of their budgets. This represents about one-third of the investment of the ninety-five departements. If the trend continues, the management of services (notably health) and the distribution of grants to rural areas will more and more become concentrated in the départements; regional government will become the centre of economic development — in particular in urban areas — and finance for large-scale capital projects. All the government had to do to prepare for this possibility was to keep out of the debate about the merits of regions versus départements. France now has four levels of government, excluding the institutions of co-operation among them, such as *syndicats de communes*, districts and *communautés urbaines*.

Conclusion

This paper has identified the role of local government in the provision of basic services (health, education and transport, for example), and in the formulation and implementation of public policy. Of course, any explanation for this degree of influence must lie in the attempt by both bureaucracy and government to centralize and control everything, without having the means to implement their decisions. Local authorities have managed to turn the complexities of the bureaucratic system to their advantage and create their own room for manoeuvre: the central state may be omnipresent, but it is also often powerless under the burden of its own weight. Similarly, the mix of roles has furthered the osmosis between centre and periphery: administrators become involved in politics, and politicians in administration. Nationally elected representatives also speak for the 'grass roots' and localism runs throughout the system, to the top. This confusion is a source of complexity, sluggishness and endless red tape. But it also has positive effects: it avoids ruptures in the policy process by promoting exchange and communication; by nationalizing local affairs, and by the special consideration accorded to peripheral interests by the national authorities. The expansion of the regional level of government and electoral reform are likely to disturb this, yet it is impossible to predict all their consequences.

7

Italy

Enzo Sanantonio

Introduction

Local government in Italy has experienced significant changes in the past fifteen years. Above all, the development of regional government has served to modify the traditional picture of a highly centralized state. Yet despite such changes, the fundamental structure of local government still bears the stamp given it by laws almost one hundred years old. This is all the more remarkable because so many other institutions have undergone radical change in the transition from the Monarchy to the fascist regime, to the Republic.

The basic framework for local government in Italy can be found in legislation passed in 1911, 1915 and 1934. The first two laws were inspired by the legal system of the Kingdom of Piedmont, which was extended to cover the whole country after national unification in 1861. In turn, this system was based on the 'uniform' model of local administration devised during the French Revolution and the Napoleonic period. The law of 1934 was passed at the height of Mussolini's regime, which had little regard for local government.

The basic system of local government comprises two levels, the commune and the province, both of which are acknowledged in the 1947 Constitution. The commune is by far the more important in functional terms. Moreover, their small size and long historical tradition have helped to generate a high degree of citizen identification.

The number of communes has remained largely unchanged since 1864, when there were 7700. This rose to 9144 in 1921, but fell to 7310 in 1931 as a result of a law passed in 1927. Their numbers have since slowly increased, reaching 8088 in 1983. The high total suggests a large number of small communes, given the size and population of the country: 58 per cent of communes have fewer than 3100 inhabitants, 88 per cent fewer than 10,000, and almost 99 per cent fewer than 65,000.

The majority of the very smallest communes, the *comuni polvere* (speck of dust communes), are to be found in the north of Italy. Although the communes are so diverse, their legal framework is based on the 'principle of uniformity', which means that all communes, whether they have 300 or 300,000 inhabitants, have the same functions and the same regulatory framework. One exception to the principle of uniformity can be found in the conduct of elections. In communes of fewer than 5000 inhabitants, there is a majority system; where the population is larger there is a d'Hondt system of proportional representation.

There are ninety-five provinces, and despite the fact that they are larger than the communes, they clearly play a secondary role. Again inherited from the distant, pre-republican past, they were endowed with boundaries that usually resulted from earlier military requirements. From the beginning, they served central government's need to co-ordinate the periphery horizontally and vertically in the same way the French prefect did. In this way, the province's own local administration, as well as central state field services within the provinces, effectively merged into a single administration; this comprised central government 'direct' administration, co-ordinated by the prefect (which still exists in a modified form), and the 'autarchic' administration of the local province, which, if only in an indirect way, also looked after the interests of the state. This trend towards the merger of state and provincial government became especially marked during the fascist period, when elections for the office of provincial president were discontinued (a fate also shared by the office of mayor).

The recent creation of regional institutions and the reduction in central government functions have sharply curtailed the prefect's role, and with it the majority of functions performed at the provincial level. The province as a local body, therefore, in return for the autonomy won from the tutelage of the prefect, more or less took on the same status as the commune: it was left without any hierarchical superiority over the communes and, above all, with a narrow range of functions of only limited importance.

Province and commune are similar in their internal organization. Both have a council (*consiglio*) elected every five years, and an executive body (*giunta*) formed from the council; and in addition, the communes have a president (*sindaco*). The provincial electoral system is based on electoral college and single nominee — in a rather original, if complicated, form — using the criterion of proportional representation.

A third, optional type of local government has been added to the two older ones. A 1976 law introduced another exception to the principle of uniformity by allowing communes to decide whether or not to divide into districts (*circoscrizioni* or *quartieri*) and, where the commune has more than 40,000 inhabitants, to decide whether the district councils (*consigli di quartiere*) should be elected by direct vote — and thereby be endowed both with consultative and decision-making powers — or by indirect suffrage, with consultative powers only.

Although the commune and the province are the basic local government units, there are several joint organizations for the provision of local services. They include the consortia (*consorzi*) for towns and the mountain communities (*comunita montane*), established in 1971 to deal with the specific problems of communes in mountainous areas. In addition, there are the catchment areas (*comprensori*), which were introduced by regional laws in the mid-1970s for development and planning purposes. They vary in size, tasks and status (that is, whether they are regional bodies or consortia of communes), according to provisions made by individual regions. More recently, the 664 local health authorities (*unita sanitarie locali* — USL), through which the communes administer hospital services in accordance with the 1978 health reform, were set up with a measure of administrative autonomy. USLs may be associations of smaller communes or comprise some or all of the larger ones.

In addition, there is, of course, the active presence within the communes of central government and the region. Their role is not confined to planning, formulating guidelines and co-ordinating. Rather, they carry out managerial and administrative functions and maintain an appropriate bureaucratic apparatus. The continuing presence at local level of the state and regional networks — which often usurp or duplicate the functions of the provinces and communes — is a curious feature of subnational government in Italy.

The state has its own local offices, which are recognized in the 1947 Constitution. Moreover, the devolution of state activity to the regions since 1970 has not meant a reduction in central government field offices. It has been estimated, in the absence of official figures, that there are about one hundred local offices of central government, each with a large staff, within each province.

Once functions have been devolved to them by the state, the regions have largely tended to hold on to those functions instead of passing them on to local government. For the regions, this has meant a heavy administrative load, an increase in bureaucracy, and a blurring of the co-ordinating role that regional legislation is supposed to perform.

The structure of subnational institutions in Italy points to the existence of a vast network of autonomous local institutions, suggesting a complete decentralization at all levels. Yet this network coexists with some important factors that reduce local government autonomy and indicate a relatively high degree of centralization.

The functions of local government
The functions of local government in Italy have progressively increased, especially over the past ten years. This is not surprising, given the great expansion in the forms, as well as the levels of state intervention brought about by the introduction of the welfare state. In the past, however, the expansion of government functions has not always led to an increase in local services. There was a tendency — especially marked during the fascist era — for the state to create new

functional agencies and ad hoc bodies as agents of service delivery, rather than use the existing local authorities.

What are the functions of local government in Italy? The 1934 law on the communes and provinces does not define the functions of local organizations, or even indicate what they are, but rather offers a long and detailed list of expenditure (often for individual activities) by communes and provinces considered obligatory. This aspect of the law demonstrates a concern with accounting, rather than an interest in specifying areas of local autonomy or in dividing functions between central and local government. The clearly subordinate status of local organizations gives them a mainly instrumental role in delivering services on behalf of the central state. As if to confirm the lack of interest in setting out functions, the 1934 law states immediately after the list of obligatory spending that 'expenditure not listed in the previous article is optional', as long as it is incurred in providing services for the benefit of the locality. A 1925 law granted communes and provinces the right to decide whether to take on the management of public services even in fields not included as obligatory expenditure in the 1934 law, for example, transport, pharmacies and public notices, often run by special municipal enterprises or managed directly by the local administration; this pointed to a sort of general right of local government to take up any functions it wished, since the sectors listed were not mandatory and the authorities were able to identify others.

However, the fact that spending on some functions is optional should not be regarded as a sure sign of decentralization in itself. Functions, whether obligatory or optional, retain exclusively local characteristics and/or the nature of an agency for the state, and so do not indicate the transfer to local government of functions typical of the centre.

The commune, rather than the province, has the more important functions. Thus, the nature of local functions, as well as their allocation, appears to be related in large measure to the 'fragmentation' of the local government system and to the small size of most communes. The subordinate nature of local government must be borne in mind when considering the wide range of matters for which the communes, according to the general legislation, have some responsibility. These matters include general administration (registration of births, marriages and deaths; demographic reporting, and statistical services); public safety and justice (a minor role); education and culture (but only in an indirect way, as local support for national functions that even today belong to central government — for example, the provision of buildings, rather than the management or remuneration of staff); local police hygiene and health (but not hospitals); social welfare (but only ancillary functions for abandoned children, the poor and the handicapped), public works, and agriculture. Only in the 1940s did legislation begin to change this general picture, bringing wider functions to the communes, for example, in public works and services, town planning, building control and infrastructure development.

The province's decision-making powers are limited in terms of range of function as well as issues connected with those functions. The fact that its territory is coextensive with that of the prefecture highlights the province's instrumental and subordinate character. Its areas of decision making include: general administration as an agent of the central state; education (provision of classrooms); public health; social welfare and benefits (psychiatric hospitals and help for the disadvantaged); public works (roads), and pest control.

The 1947 Constitution does not throw any direct light on functions. Nor does it elaborate a principle for dividing decision making between the state and the local authorities through some general clause, or in the form of a list of functions (only for the regions are some matters guaranteed), and it accepts the existing pattern of local government in the provinces and communes. The constitution showed faith in the rapid transformation of many features of Italian government, including local administration. However, the first election results, and the governments that followed, led to a kind of constitutional 'freeze', of which one of the most obvious features was the failure to implement regionalization. With it, therefore, the principles introduced by the constitution relating to 'territorial authorities' — conceived as a unitary system characterized by the innovatory presence of the regions — could have little operative effect. What did develop was a 'truncated' system. Although the constitution stated that 'the regions normally exercise their administrative functions by delegating them to local authorities', and thus offered the prospect of an expansion in local government services, these new functions failed to emerge.

The sectoral legislation that followed the 1947 Constitution was in line with this general thrust. Although local government functions did expand in the next twenty years, this involved no qualitative change in the role of local authorities in service delivery and merely confirmed their subordination to central government. Functions in some important areas, such as construction, town planning, pollution, *Mezzogiorno* (development in the south), hospitals and infant schools, were to be instrumental and dependent on the central state. For example, in matters of land use, the communes draw up their own plans in the light of rules and standards set out by central government; in the construction field, the communes decide where to build and do the construction, but planning and finance are left to the centre.

The failure to implement regionalization, as well as the local authorities' relative lack of involvement in the general growth in public functions, contributed during the 1950s and 1960s to the wider picture of the kind of nominal decentralization, almost devoid of meaning, typical of a unitary centralized state. The importance of this subordinate role of local government is its longevity: its governing norms and features remained to create a particularly burdensome inheritance for proponents of regionalization in the 1970s.

Regional reform in the 1970s marked the abandonment of centralism and the shift towards a new form of state based on autonomous local organizations. This change formed the basis for a redistribution of functions between central and local government. Yet everything that took place after 1970 — even the expansion in local government functions — was grafted on to the system defined in 1934, creating delicate problems of compatibility between the old and the new. In order to understand how the functions of the local authorities were expanded, one needs to refer to the transfer of functions in 1977. The guiding principle — that of completing the previous transfer according to a principle of 'organically linked sectors' — drew a sharper distinction between central and regional functions.

For the local authorities, the concept of 'organically linked' sectors meant that when a sufficiently coherent block of functions had been detached from the central administration, functions of 'exclusively local interest' within this block should be handed over to the provinces, communes and other local organizations. It was thought that this would also provide a solution to another problem: the reluctance shown by the regions to delegate functions to lower levels of government. This has caused a measure of friction in relationships between the regions and other local authorities, because it gives the latter some former regional services and, to some degree, takes authority away from the regions. In addition, it has helped to revive the previously close relations between local and central government, in a kind of perverse affinity. Nevertheless, the fact remains that the state, through bypassing the regions, has clearly broadened the functional sphere of the local authorities.

Important examples of the way the state has bypassed the regions include legislation on professional training, tourism, transport and health. The 1978 law reforming the health services has given new importance to the local authorities by allocating to them the major responsibility for hospital services. This and similar laws have also tidied up the subnational government system to some extent, by regrouping functions or doing away with apparently redundant national or local organizations — those whose functions had been

regionalized, or that belonged to the older forms of mutual assurance
— thus finally winning back part of the ground lost some decades ago.

Such a change does not mean, however, that the general expansion
in local government functions depends exclusively on the state's
attitude towards local government. Nor would it be correct to suggest
that all the regions have refused to delegate functions to local government. On the contrary, some have passed innovative legislation of the
highest quality, setting out imaginative organizational solutions,
structures and functions, thus anticipating the general legislation of
the state itself, which, in many cases, needed only to extend to the
whole country what a few 'pilot' regions had pioneered. This
enterprising spirit was reflected in the creation of new intermediate
levels — comprehensive districts (*comprensori*) — above the
communes, as a means of co-ordinating planning. If, in some cases,
this has appeared to reveal distrust and antagonism towards the local
authorities that were bypassed (for example, the *comprensorio*
usurped the province), in others it has been less open to criticism; this
is because it provoked reflection on the problem of the size and
number of communes, and indicating new ways of improving the
relationship between size and function in the local authorities. The
expansion in local government functions therefore owes much to these
regional experiments.

The overall picture that appears at this point is particularly
complex. It is sufficient to note that the regulations governing the
local authorities are scattered throughout state legislation passed
during this century, and still in force in regional legislation. In the
absence of a law or some other formal document setting out the
functions of the local authorities, we can use the concept of
'organically linked sectors' to illustrate the allocation of responsibilities between different levels of government. A study entitled
'Inquiry into the Functions of Local Authorities in Italy', recently
conducted by the Institute for Regional Studies, Rome, examined
organically linked sectors that can in turn be subdivided into almost
300 separate activities. By exploring how many are performed by each
level of government in four regions — Abruzzi, Lombardy, Sicily and
Tuscany — we are able to split the functions into four main groups.
The first comprises those where the local authorities have
responsibility for most of the activities within the sector. Thus the
communes have the main responsibility for the local police;
registration of births, marriages and deaths, demographic reporting,
statistical services; hygiene of soil and dwellings; justice and taxes,
and safeguarding the environment from pollution. The USLs have
major responsibility for health. Second, there are areas best described
as shared between the communes and the regions, as both make

significant contributions to these sectors. They include town planning; social welfare, and public housing and reconstruction. Third, there are sectors that are best described as shared between regions, communes and provinces (or mountain communities). These include civil defence; roads; expropriation; public works, and protection of the land. Fourth, there are sectors in which the region has an over-riding or strong presence. These include professional training; craft industry; public land and possessions; transport; fairs and monuments; agriculture and environmental protection; water resources; industry, and tourism.

TABLE 1
Italy: local government's share of public expenditure, 1970–81
(Per cent)

	Central government	Regions	Provinces	Communes
1970	70	3	5	23
1975	64	12	4	21
1981	64	19	2	14

Source: Instituto Centrale di Statistica (ISTAT), *Annuario Statistico Italiano*, Rome, various years.

This distribution of functions enables the provinces to spend relatively little (2 per cent of public expenditure in 1981), leaving the regions (19 per cent) with a higher share than communes (14 per cent), but it is important that lists of functions and tables of spending figures should not be interpreted in such a way as to produce a distorted and misleading picture (see Table 1). It is also important to understand what functions exist and how many are performed by each organization, and, from wider viewpoint, to realize that the functions are carried out by all the bodies at the same time and in the same arena, competing, overlapping and interacting with each other, creating flexible networks for policy making and implementation. This complex pattern is impossible to unravel, and cannot be set out in a neat and ordered scheme. The rigid elements within it, such as formal responsibilities and hierarchical powers, tend not to be absolute, but combine with the more flexible ones, such as widespread participation in policy-making processes and broad sharing of responsibilities. This results not only from force of circumstance, but from legal provisions that have introduced various forms of linkage among different levels of government, such as mixed committees and organizations, joint opinions and procedures. The limited scope of exclusive responsibility for any level of government has generated a model based less on the separation between levels of government as on their interdependence and integration.

Discretion

If discretion means 'freedom from others', one might be tempted to conclude from the evidence presented so far that it is difficult to speak of discretion in the existing tangle of subnational government in Italy. The question of whether the local authorities can be presumed to be omnicompetent is an open one, as there is no specific legal ruling that makes explicit reference to omnicompetence. Nevertheless, the provisions for optional expenditure, and the fact that the local authorities are allowed to provide public services at their discretion, means that they are effectively omnicompetent. Local authorities do perform functions which are strictly ultra vires in the sense that they do not appear in formal legislation, yet the authorities have not been challenged on the legality of their actions.

However, the possibility of expanding into sectors of choice, provided they are of public service, does constitute a potential for autonomy that can only be realized if there are sufficient resources to finance the services chosen by local communes.

The traditional impact of prescriptive laws and regulations that determine functions, individual activities and their content in minute fashion, plus an increase in the volume of regulation that has accompanied the development of the welfare state, means that 'optional' functions are becoming less important, and that much more of what local government does is taken up by functions that are explicitly defined in legislation.

On the other hand, the fact that provision is explicit does not always mean it is obligatory. Often there exist no real sanctions against non-provision of a mandatory service, because the system of controls is geared towards preventing illegal actions by the local authorities rather than compelling them to do things. Indeed, services may not be carried out for a variety of reasons; they may be beyond the scope of small communes, or political leaders may see little electoral advantage in them. Although one is forced to recognize the marginal influence of optional functions, the fact remains that the others are not always truly obligatory.

One further dimension to the nature of local discretion is related not to the question of whether to act, but of how to act. Laws do not normally limit themselves to identifying a function and allocating it to a specific level of local government, leaving the local administration to determine in detail how the function should be provided. Instead, laws are often detailed to the point where they predetermine the content of a service and the way in which it is delivered. In this situation, little is left to the discretion of the local authority. The margins of discretion in this regard are not firm and guaranteed, but haphazard; they are always directly dependent on the detail and restrictions embodied in any particular legislation, whether regional or state law. Thus, each area of local government activity constitutes, as it were, a separate subsystem, with its own pattern of institutional relationships and a different balance of power between the different levels of government. In broad terms, one can say in some cases there is a prevailing regional influence (even where central government structures survive), and in these cases the balance is in favour of local government. This happens, for example, in newly developed services, such as tourism, which are largely decentralized and regionalized, and in which interests are rooted and defended at the local level. In other cases, the centre has a dominating influence and the balance tilts to the side of central government. This tends to occur in matters where, despite widespread decentralization of functions, a high degree of state control of important decision making persists, and the influence of the national level is reinforced by the nature of the relevant interest groups, which are organized on a national basis. This is the case, for example, with the health service, where, as far as autonomy of direction and co-ordination are concerned, the minister has actually regained and increased his powers, leaving the regions to participate on a consultative basis, with no real influence over decisions. The same can be said of agriculture, where the extremely strong influence of European Economic Community policies brings about an overall upward shift in political responsibility and an expansion in the role of the minister as representative of the country's interests. Here, and especially in health, it is evident that centralization occurs at the expense of the region, since, given their size, the smaller local authorities could hardly aspire to a significant role in policy making, yet have considerable responsibility for service delivery and administration.

There is a third pattern of relationship displaying a high degree of centralization; this occurs when the regions are displaced to the sidelines by the establishment of direct links between the centre and the localities, in which the latter's role is more passive than active. This often takes the form of a direct (and welcome) relationship of a financial kind between the minister and the communes. Such a relationship bypasses the regions and mediates the conflict between them and local authorities. This happens, for example, with public building. In such cases, the recently formed joint organizations, committees and other forms of participation and co-ordination tend to represent mechanisms that lead to a greater degree of involvement by the centre, instead of generating truly active and equal participation in decision making. Thus they allow the higher echelons in the ministries to recover, at the policy and general decision-making level, a measure of power to shape the broad content of policy; this is comparable with the 'hands on' administrative power that they lost in the devolution process. Central government achieves better results by these methods, and through the legislation and agreements that they generate, than it does by using the normal channels and means of influence, such as circulars, directives and similar ordinances, which exist alongside the joint bodies.

The changes in local government's relation with the centre, accelerated by the regionalization process, have brought about a marked diminution in the role of the prefect from the time when his influence was unchallenged in every area of local activity. This influence was not simply a question of hierarchical command. At the beginning of the century, the office of prefect was that of an intermediary. Apart from controlling local administration on the basis of his legal powers, he represented the interests of local community and transmitted local views to central government. A similar system of direct and widespread general supervision on the part of central government no longer exists. The description given by communal and provincial law to the office of prefect — that he or she is a 'representative in the province of the power of the executive' — still applies, but has been stripped of much of its meaning.

Nevertheless, the prefect has retained some responsibilities, and these allow his or her presence to be felt in the work of the local authorities, above all in the communes and provinces. The prefect has some general powers, such as the power to collect, arrange and transmit information; to scrutinize 'the actions of all public bodies', and to adopt, 'should urgent necessity require it, the measure indispensable for the public interest in the different branches of the service.' Other duties, such as the right to inspect the functions of mayors as government officials rather than as heads of municipal councils, are more limited and narrowly defined. The prefect acts as an agent of the state in functions such as the registration of births, deaths and marriages; public health; public safety and order; municipal building; local police, and veterinary inspection. Here, he or she has the power to issue emergency decrees. In cases of default, the prefect can delegate a commissioner to carry out those duties that the mayor has failed to fulfil. In such cases, the prefect has real control over public organizations. Similarly, he or she has powers to intervene in cases where the mayoral office has lapsed, been abolished or suspended, as well as the power to summon, suspend or dissolve municipal and provincial councils. Furthermore, the prefect's role was extended in 1981 in the fields of civil defence and public order, and in co-ordinating the smaller local bodies through an advisory technical and legal service. It is difficult at present to establish precisely the significance of the prefect's role. However, it appears still to be relatively minor.

Another way of assessing the effective room for local discretion is to examine the nature of central control. At present, the central state can make its influence felt at lower levels both by exercising its administrative functions and through various other direct administrative channels, such as the various forms of joint co-operation and the office of prefect. Yet the centre no longer has the general power to control the local authorities' administrative activity. Regional reform, in fact, has led to an important change of emphasis in the system of local government, bringing into effect a provision in the Republican constitution of 1947 that stated that the regions were to 'exercise control over the actions of the provinces, the communes and other local authorities.' The organizations that exercise effective control — regional committees of control (Co. Re. Co.) — are decentralized. In each region there are, alongside a single committee for the provinces and USLs, various departments that exercise control over the communes and other local authorities, including consortia, mountain communes, comprehensive districts and regional agencies.

Nevertheless, despite having been 'regionalized', the system of control is still formally as it was in the nineteenth century. The old model has been maintained. It is, in fact, a model based on legal inspection of all the individual administrative actions of each authority. With one or two exceptions, approval is needed to make these actions legal. It is true that the control over the substance of decisions, as opposed to their legality, is now much lighter, taking the form of simple referral of the decision back to the authority. Nevertheless, the controls remain very similar to those the prefect had at his disposal, and which allowed him to keep a close and constant check on local government. The only formal innovation, appears to be the change of controller; the position of the local authorities remains one of strict subordination, even if the superior authority is now the region. This suggests a high degree of continuity in the system of control.

On the basis of the formal position, one must conclude that the local authorities are supervised in a very detailed way, and that their powers of discretion are small. But here, too, it is important to consider the way in which controls actually function. It is clear that, although the rules have not changed, their transposition to a radically different context — regionalization and decentralization — does constitute an important element of change and opens the way for further development. It is also doubtful whether rules and instruments conceived for the office of prefect — monocratic, hierarchical and isolated from the centre — can be as easily applied to different purposes, especially when it is remembered that the object of control itself has changed because of the massive qualitative and quantitative shift in local government activity. Hundreds of thousands of by-laws are put before each committee every year; a single enactment is no longer important in itself, but in relation to the totality of functions, services and strategies.

Methods of control have clearly been adapted to the new environment. However, given that the formal features remain unchanged, this spontaneous adaptation has occurred in such a manner as to provoke serious distortions in the ways controls are exercised, as well as in the purposes of this control. This has compromised not so much the autonomy of local government, but rather the validity and effectiveness of this channel for supervising the local authorities. The control has changed its nature to such an extent that it is now entirely part of a political network. It has been observed that control is exercised when sanction and validity are given to agreements reached by local political forces, or when a veto is sought as another means of exerting influence on decisions taken by others. It can also be effective where there are powers to block decisions that may be accepted as legal elsewhere. In addition, control organizations can be used by their members to cultivate a political party or set of interests and to build careers for themselves.

The spread and political colouring of the members of these control bodies (both those appointed by the regional council and those not openly politicized) goes beyond the traditional pattern of 'dividing the spoils'. The controllers, a good proportion of whom are chosen from political personnel, regardless of competence or qualification, are seen as relatively autonomous centres of politico-administrative power who with rare exceptions, represent their own interests or, at most, those of a political party. The committees certainly do not represent the state or the region.

It is therefore of fundamental importance to understand that these controls — in the way they have been implemented by law, and by their very nature — are not a regional instrument. Despite the fact that the constitution speaks of committees as 'an organ of the Region', their fragmentation in structure and conduct means that they are not directed by any single centre, be it regional or at any other level. Each is highly individual and as a set they are ungovernable. Fragmentation and randomness in the exercise of control contrasts with the uniform treatment and objectivity that their position as representatives of a legal order might lead one to expect.

Financial relationships offer another means by which local

discretion may be narrowed. In the past twenty years, these relationships have undergone substantial change. Here again, events that occurred at the beginning of the regionalization process, and during its subsequent development, are important. The revenue sources of the two major substate bodies, the region and the commune, are set out in Table 2.

TABLE 2
Italy: revenues of ordinary statute regions and communes, 1972—80
(Per cent distribution)

| | 1972 | | 1976 | | 1980 | |
	Regions	Communes	Regions	Communes	Regions	Communes
Tax revenues	11.6	15.6	3.9	3.6	1.6	6.0
Borrowing	—	67.3	4.1	69.6	0.7	27.8
Other own-source revenues	0.8	6.8	2.7	6.2	1.7	7.5
Central govt. transfers	87.6	10.3	89.3	20.6	96.0	58.7
Total	100.0	100.0	100.0	100.0	100.0	100.0

Source: E. Buglione and G. France: 'Skewed Fiscal Federalism in Italy. Implications for Public Expenditure and Control', in A. Prenchand and J. Burkhead (eds): *Comparative International Budgeting and Finance*, New Brunswick/London: Transaction Books, 1984.

By 1980, the position differed from that which obtained before the regional reform. Until 1972, local government finance was characterized by a high degree of autonomy. Tax receipts and borrowing levels in the communes (equivalent to 15.6 and 67.3 per cent of income, respectively) were substantially higher than transfers from central government (10.3 per cent) and allowed real freedom to finance optional expenditure. Local authorities also made extensive use of bank loans. Regionalization followed an important phase in the organization of local government finance. At the same time functions were decentralized, central government decided to introduce a radical centralization of the financial system. There have been many different interpretations of this, ranging from the purely technical — the need to introduce tax reforms to bring the Italian system into line with those of its European partners — to the more clearly political: the centre's desire to retain control and influence in the face of the unknowns of regionalization. A variety of factors shaped the centralization of finance, but the results have had an extremely important effect on the local government system.

Central government almost entirely took over the business of resource allocaton with the full agreement of the political elites, all of which were advocating a fairer system of taxation. Local taxes were abolished, except for a few minor ones, such as those on health resorts, holiday makers and tourists, dog owners, advertising, notices and refuse collection, plus building licences. As a result, revenue from local taxation collapsed (down to 3.6 per cent in 1976), as Table 2 shows. To compensate for this reduction in income, the state provided equivalent funds rising annually by up to 10 per cent (in fact the sums doubled in 1976). On the other hand, a new local tax — but levied and collected by the state on the increase in the value of property (INVIM), calculated at the change of ownership — did not bring any appreciable benefits to the local authorities. Another new tax, on income from property and self-employment (ILOR), again collected by the state, did not lead to the intended distribution to regions, provinces, communes and other local bodies. Even though the borrowing option remained open to them after the abolition of the requirement that they balance budgets, the local authorities began to depend heavily on central government for resources — a situation that continues today.

At the same time, demand for public goods and services increased: it was in the 1970s that the expansion took place in functions that accompanied and characterized decentralization. To this may be added the results of the 1975 election, which led to the takeover of most large local authorities by left-wing coalitions, upsetting the traditional patterns of local politics. In the economic sphere, inflationary stresses set in that brought about a substantial increase in expenditure, as well as a reduction in local authority income in real terms. If various other negative effects are taken into account — from rigidifying income, given the loss of any local flexibility in taxation, to the occasional ceilings imposed on charges for local services — one can understand why the local authorities were passing through one of their bleakest periods. Decentralization coincided with a serious economic crisis.

Seeking a way out of the impasse, the local authorities yielded more of their autonomy in exchange for additional resources, in the form of grants; in 1976, these reached 20.6 per cent of local income. At the same time, they used their few remaining instruments to increase their resources, and in this way attempted to revive their autonomy in some areas. This resulted in persistent recourse by the majority of communes to the money markets, as the consistently high level of borrowing shows — it was equivalent to 69.6 per cent of income in 1976; this was not only to finance investments but to cover deficits, even though this gave a further twist to the vicious spiral whereby some authorities increased their current deficit to make good previous ones. All this took place under the complaisant eye of a central government preoccupied by the fierce social tensions of those years.

The expansion in local welfare functions, in conjunction with the financial crisis, led to closer intergovernmental relationships. A relative decline in the autonomy of local government became evident. Also apparent was local subordination to the discretionary powers of the region, where the latter was charged with distributing state funds. Faced with the chaos engendered by increasing deficits, central government in 1977 decided to intervene in a different way. It accepted the burden of writing off the debts incurred by the local authorities, abolished their power to borrow for current expenditure, set strict limits on spending increases (especially for personnel), introduced the requirement to balance the budget, and guaranteed additional transfers where ordinary income proved insufficient. These provisions represent further limitations on the financial autonomy of the local authorities. This is not only because of a large percentage drop in borrowing since 1976 (more than halved, and equivalent in 1980 to 27.8 per cent of income) and the persistently small contribution from their own tax sources (only 5.7 per cent), but because of the corresponding decisive increase in central government transfers (58.7 per cent), which have become by far the largest single source of local income. However, it must be added that the grants are largely block grants, with no conditions attached.

The role of the state is quite different from that of the regions. Regional income is also derived from the state, without any appreciable autonomy. But the region, in turn, passes on a large part of the resources so received (87 per cent in 1982) to other organizations (63.9 per cent to local health groups; 9.5 per cent to private companies; 7.8 per cent to public bodies; 4.2 per cent to public enterprises; 1.6 per cent to families, and 0.8 per cent to central administration), including some area bodies (12.3 per cent went to communes, provinces, mountain communes and consortia).

Transfers to the local authorities — mainly for social services, land and building — are not negligible. Nevertheless, they do not allow the region to exert effective powers of control over the communes and provinces, because the sums transferred remain a modest fraction of their income, compared with the much greater receipts from the state and from borrowing. The most the region can do is to see that the money is spent on the goods and services it specifies; in general, it has no powers of decision about policy co-ordination. This is perhaps because the region's financial relationships with communes and provinces are too weak; this contrasts with the position of the USLs, for which regional transfers are almost the only source of income. Financial relationships between the local authorities and the state are much closer, as we have seen. However, given that it is impossible for the centre to supervise all local authority budgets, it might well have been able to provide some useful role for the region that took account of its position and included it in the financial system between central and local government. Instead, power was delegated to the provincial sections of the regional committees of control; these already have a heavy responsibility for supervising local decision making and, despite all the problems this can lead to, are the only organizations charged with checking that local authority budgets conform to the complex legal requirements set out by central government. Nor does the region yet have more general powers, for example, control over local investment policy, any substantial responsibility for local financial planning, or any control over access to credit.

It is in the area of finance, therefore, that one can most easily grasp the dynamics of the relationships between the central state and local government. The close relationship between them has also been revealed in the analysis of the distribution of functions and of other features relating to discretion. All this confirms the fact that central and local government have a mutual interest in maintaining these direct channels, which bypass the region.

The regions' weak influence on intergovernmental financial relations serves merely to underline the pervasive presence of central government in ways quite different from the ordinary forms of control. In financial terms alone, this gives the Italian system an extreme and singular position compared with other countries. Given this, it is difficult to speak of real local autonomy, although the growth in local spending and the unconditional nature of central grants mean some discretion remains in the allocation of spending to different services.

Access
One final way to assess the degree of decentralization is by evaluating the institutional weight local government can bring to bear on national policy making through various forms of access to central government.

Several aspects of access patterns have already emerged. The combined effects of the presence of many levels of local government and the fragmented division of functions among them, the ways in which controls on local authorities actually function, and the direct channels for financing services — are all features that entail, in different ways, frequent occasions for discussion, conflict and close contact between central and local government, and help to create a complicated institutional tangle. In addition, patterns of access have features more directly related to the political system. Such features tend to escape measurement, not least because of their informal character; even the literature is relatively thin on this matter. The long tradition of studies on political parties at the national level has almost no counterpart — with one or two exceptions — for local politics; we have no general picture of the interactions between parties and trades unions at the local level, or of the contacts between the local authorities.

It would be as well to start from two premises: the existence of mass parties and the high degree of politicization in Italian society. Given the longstanding importance and dominance of these features of Italian politics, it is likely that they can provide the key to an understanding of the modes of access to, and effective power that local factors can exert on central departments. It remains to identify the place of local institutions within this general political context.

In terms of the party system, there has been since the 1970s a considerable growth of local government in the context of the wider expansion in public services. It is important to consider the effects of this process of expansion on local government organization. The 8088 communes each have one mayor and provide a total 103,631 council members and 39,913 councillors. The ninety-five provinces each have one president, and there is a total 2035 council members and 701 councillors in charge of departments. Alongside these traditional substate bodies are the twenty-two regions and autonomous provinces, with 1000 or so council members; there are also 348 mountain communities and 664 local health authorities, which, with 500 municipal enterprises, have 28,000 administrators. The consortia and districts have about another 1500. Furthermore, decentralization, by extending the powers of the local authorities, has also increased the number of organizations and the activities controlled by them. For example, 154,000 administrators are appointed locally, of a total of about 400,000 for the 41,000 public organizations of various kinds — economic bodies that deliver services, administrative organizations and so-called 'parastate' bodies. This is no different to the way in which thousands of other administrative agencies are split between development authorities, regional enterprises, regional and local finance companies, tourism and holiday enterprises.

In addition, the communes have the right to elect their own representatives to myriad joint bodies and committees operating in various sectors, from building to employment. Local representatives also have a significant presence, with party and trades union officials, in cultural, leisure and sporting organizations, and in the thousands of agricultural co-operatives.

The panorama, of course, could be made more detailed, but it does give an idea of how diffuse the local authorities are and how, apart from administering about one-third of the national budget and 1.5 million employees, they have considerable political power. At the same time, it is clear that the local authorities' decision-making bodies are composed of party political elements (elected basically according to the principle of proportional representation) and, in choosing their representatives, do so on party lines; even the USLs, for example, are run exclusively along party lines. Thus local authorities and political parties can in very complex ways — it is frequently impossible to tell which loyalty prevails from one occasion to the next in the behaviour of the appointed representatives — expand wholesale through these multiple networks of power.

The local authorities are therefore channels through which the political parties operate. At the same time, the opposite is also true: the authorities themselves have much to gain through party political channels. The party system, in fact, has always been present in central administration and affiliated organizations, from credit institutions to public enterprises. Decentralization and regionalization, which the parties themselves advocated because they offered new areas of control and fresh outlets for an expanding group of professional politicians, have further helped to integrate political forces within all the administrative structures and public organizations, allowing them to extend their network of influence. The parties are now deeply rooted within the system and pervade public activity to such a point that complaints about a 'spoils system' and of the parties taking over all aspects of public life are common. Party links are important, and the party system — for good or evil — appears to be the connecting tissue, the general binding force on all institutions.

From this perspective, the parties appear to have a fairly centralized organization in many ways, and decentralization and regionalization have had limited impact on this centralization. Such a centralized system is credited by many with holding together the bits and pieces of an institutional framework that is otherwise so fragmented that it would be almost impossible to administer. The very marginality of strictly local parties (often tailored to the specific problems of a single commune, like the 'civic lists') serves to confirm the strong overall hold that the party system has on even the most local of authorities. According to figures from the 1979 and 1980 elections, 77.7 per cent of council members belong to a national party; 12.9 per cent are sympathizers; 7.2 per cent are 'independents', often elected on party list, and only 2.3 per cent belong to ethnic, linguistic or other groups. This can result in the centre exerting a strong influence on the issues at stake in local elections: even so-called 'administrative' elections may be rendered 'political', with national questions — defined by the parties — displacing concrete and specifically local issues.

On the other hand, centralization through the political parties' local government policy sections seems fairly limited. It mainly concerns large local authorities, for which coalition options are assessed and decided at party headquarters, because they are an important part of the wider game of national politics. Smaller local authorities are usually untouched by these moves. Conversely, factors of potential centralization are in some measure counterbalanced by the ways in which political parties depend on the local authorities — and not only on the large and important ones. The fact that politicians are elected at national and regional level from constituencies with similar boundaries — large communes and provinces — means they must bear in mind the interests of their electorate. Moreover, local authorities are often the source of hidden finance from which the party apparatus, even at the national level, draws resources to meet rising costs. For obvious reasons, figures are not available, but it is estimated that declared contributions to party funds comprise only a very small part of their income.

Although the parties have strong national features, they are not a constant force for centralization, and they make the channels of communication between central and local government accessible to two-way traffic, often with equal chances of success. To this extent, local and national politicians — those in local and national government, plus 25,000-30,000 party functionaries — may act as links in a single chain of transmission between central and local government. On this basis, central government is fairly permeable to partisan influence from below.

Links of this kind allow the attainment, in more informal ways, of what in other countries is achieved through institutional forms such as the *cumul des mandats*, which is expressly forbidden in Italy. The position of members of parliament is legally incompatible with that of provincial president and councillor in charge of a department, or with that of a mayor and councillor of a commune, again in charge of a department. For the rest, links are possible without membership of any particular party. The political channel between party headquarters and the various and multiple 'localisms' and 'pluralisms' is largely open, and allows access through a variety of routes according to sector, objectives, interests and the political figures involved. This too is a form of adaptation to an environment characterized by a substantial number of local coalitions of several parties: in 1982, there were 110 different combinations of major and minor parties. It also reflects the lack of consistency in local and national political alliances, and the very lack of alternation and renewal at the upper levels of central government. Such a context entails mediation, exchange and compromise. In a situation like this, it is possible for a mayor with initiative to act as policy broker and to find the proper channel for entering direct contact with the appropriate central source of decisions (Tarrow, 1977).

This potential network of relationships, on which the possibilities for manoeuvre in terms of function definition depends, is also one of the resources that a local politician can exploit to construct his *cursus honorum*. A strong local base provides a good starting point for a career. For example, in most parties a period spent gaining administrative experience with a local authority forms part of the training for many national officials. The majority of members of regional councils also have local experience.

Finally, one should not neglect another fundamental point of reference for the system of local government. For some time, the invisible presence has been felt of a 'party of local authorities' that cuts horizontally across all existing political parties and their parliamentary representatives. Although it is a force represented at the national level, it has shown a constant desire to defend and enhance the position of local government, ensuring, where necessary, a prompt and effective mobilization of forces that can be as cohesive as that provided by party organization itself.

One could not claim the same effectiveness for the mediating role of professional groups as such. To the extent that the prevailing culture and over-riding logic are political and not technocratic, these pressure groups are either weak, or less closely involved in the policy process.

In so far as they address issues of local interest, professional demands are subordinated to the demands of the political system whenever confrontation takes place. For example, although they usually represent a powerful professional and political force in other countries, in Italy doctors are practically excluded from responsibility for managing the local health authorities, which remain partisan. Professional categories, or better, single groups, may indeed find themselves working directly alongside the local authorities, as consultants for example, or be among the beneficiaries of local political decisions and administrative activity. But this is a separate issue, and the patronage it opens up underlines the importance of the professional dimension in Italian local administration, which has not avoided the general trend towards increased politicization of public office, especially since the 1970s.

The role of the administrative bureaucracies is worthy of more attention. The existence of mass parties has led not only to the parties' presence in posts that are 'political' in the strict sense, such as representative bodies and major public agencies, but also to their large-scale takeover of public administration. This phenomenon is one aspect of the logic that characterizes the division of power ('sharing the spoils') through which the political system controls so much of public life both directly and indirectly. This relatively new relationship leads to an increasing number of public life both directly and indirectly. This relatively new relationship leads to an increasing number of public employees joining party organizations. It has been estimated that between 85 and 90 per cent of party members in large communes are public-sector employees, and between 60 and 70 per cent in the rural communes. Some public employees are seconded directly to party organizations, working full time, but keeping their old jobs. Others work part-time for the party, although still fully employed by the public sector; 63 per cent of Socialist Party activists perform part-time work for the party, for example.

As a result, the position any individual occupies may be confused to the point where it becomes difficult to distinguish the administrative sphere from the political. The real risk is that a sort of 'closed' system will come to operate more and more, with large numbers of people who are employed by public (even local) administrations, but take their orders from the party. They cannot be unequivocally labelled as 'public servants', because it is no longer clear to whom they are rendering a service.

The national organizations of local government occupy an important place in central–local relations. The principal ones are the National Association of Communes (ANCI), the Union of Provinces (UPI) and the Confederation of Municipalized Firms, (CISPEL). In the past, these associations handled matters of representation and offered services to their members. They draw their strength from their wide membership and the prestige of their presidents, all of whom have been prominent figures in a major local authority. They have recently exerted even more influence at the central state level by creating an image of cohesion and consensus in their proposals for changes to policies affecting local government. This cohesion appears to be confirmed by the associations' ability to share out their presidencies among the parties — ANCI to the Christian Democrats; UPI to the Socialists, and CISPEL to the Communist Party. The associations are almost always present wherever and whenever questions of local interest are discussed, and they also have seats on many joint bodies, intergovernmental boards and consultative committees, acting as the formal representatives of the local authorities. They may exert pressure in conjunction with the parties, lobbying the government and parliament. They have scored many successes in shaping local government legislation, as well as the provisions for sharing financial resources, credit control, through

Cassa Depositi e Prestiti, and personnel policy. This national role of the associations appears to have a decentralizing effect. It is also a product of the pull exerted by the decision-making organizations of central government with which the bargaining is conducted. To this extent, the associations appear to be leading actors in the conduct of relationships between central and local government, although it should be remembered that the role is relatively new and difficult to evaluate; although they themselves operate according to centralized methods, with a national organization participating in national policy-making processes, they end up by strengthening the overall system of local government. The associations therefore constitute a channel through which local needs (in so far as they are represented and interpreted by the associations) can be put before central government. Recent confirmation of this pattern can be found in the proposals presented to parliament for the reform of local authorities, many of which bear strong 'localistic' and especially 'municipalistic' imprints. The defence of ground already won and the bypassing of the region are sure signs of the influence of national organizations at the draft stage.

Conclusions

The local government system in Italy has experienced fundamental changes in the past fifteen years or so. It is impossible to label such changes as unambiguously 'centralizing' or 'decentralizing'. Many of the old forms of central control have been abandoned or modified, only to reappear in different guises. Many of the new forms intended to achieve greater decentralization have at most only slightly altered traditional patterns of central–local interaction or, in some cases, reinforced them.

First, if the object of the exercise is to define the system of local government in its relation to the centre, the analysis reveals a complicated institutional tangle in which it is easier to identify forms of co-operation, co-management and joint endeavour than clear and sharp divisions of exclusive responsibility. Second, the Italian system is highly fluid. It represents a kaleidoscope in which the different features of various government levels, and their size and influence, can vary according to the sectors, policies and instruments in question at any one time. It is almost impossible to determine whether the system is centralized or decentralized, because features of extreme centralization co-exist with powerful decentralizing forces.

8
Spain

Thomas Clegg

Introduction: central –local relations in Spain

The evolution of central –local relations in Spain raises a number of questions distinct from those raised in other countries studied in this work. One important difference lies in the absence of representative government at either the central or local level during most of the postwar period. The nature of local government institutions within the Francoist regime and their relationship both with the local population and with the other levels of the state varied from those found in the liberal democracies of West Europe. A second difference results from the reform of the basic territorial structure of the state introduced with the transition to democracy after 1975. The devolution of important legislative and executive powers to new elected bodies at the regional level was more far-reaching than the decentralization reforms introduced during the same period in France and Italy, particularly with regard to the dominant role that the regions have been given in relation to local authorities.

The system of local government that existed in Spain at the time of General Franco's death in 1975 remained essentially the same as that set up by the Liberals in the early nineteenth century. This system, consolidated in definitive form by 1833, was based on the Napoleonic model. It swept away the rather anarchic and overlapping local jurisdictions and institutions of the Ancien Regime, replacing them with two tiers of legally uniform units that still exist today: the fifty provinces and 9000 or so municipalities (gradually reduced to 8022 by 1981 — CEUMT, 1983). These units, which correspond to the French *départements* and *communes*, have served as the territorial basis for central state organizations and for the exercise of local self-government by representative bodies. Executive powers were concentrated in the hands of monocratic figures: the civil governor (*Gobernador Civil*) at the provincial level, and the mayor (*Alcalde*) at the municipal level. Under most of the regimes since 1833, these agents have been appointed by the central government and acted simultaneously as the agents of the centre in the local areas and as the presiding heads of the local elected assemblies: the provincial council (*Diputacion*) and municipal council (*Ayuntamiento*). The municipal councillors were directly elected by residents, and councillors in turn also elected the members of the provincial body. The councils' powers were limited both in terms of their functions and through the controls exercised over their activities by the appointed executive agents.

The degree of centralism inherent in this system was exacerbated over time (Garcia de Enterría, 1972:59 – 100). Specialized field services of the central ministries, organized at the provincial level, and other technical agencies took on most of the new functions and tasks of public administration that emerged, rather than local government. Overall co-ordination of these field services and agencies was the nominal responsibility of the civil governor, but unlike the French *prefet* he remained a political appointee with little administrative expertise. The political nature of his role was reflected in his primary tasks: the maintenance of public order, the suppression of trades unions and strikes, censorship of the press, and the distribution of public funds, employment and patronage within an extended 'spoils system'. Patronage reached its peak during the Restoration period (1875 – 1923) in the form of *caciquismo*, which involved a wholesale manipulation of the electoral system through fraud, corruption and violent intimidation, in order to protect the artificial alternance in power (*torno*) of the two major monarchist parties (Liberals and Conservatives), while excluding the republican, socialist and regionalist opposition. The civil governors were key figures in these arrangements, organizing networks of political chiefs (*caciques*) and their clientele to control both local and national levels of government (Carr, 1983:366 – 78; Temime, Broder and Chastagnaret, 1982:159 – 62).

The pattern of centralized control over local institutions through such means was a crucial element in preserving the political domination of the Spanish oligarchy of aristocratic landowners and financial magnates, even after the introduction of universal manhood suffrage in 1890. But it failed to produce the political integration of the population as a whole, and was subject to repeated challenges from the opposition forces, frequently organized at the local or regional level. Municipal insurrections in 1836, 1840 and 1868 helped to bring about brief periods of progressive rule in Madrid. During the short-lived First Republic (1872 – 75), an attempt was made at establishing a federal constitution. The first years of the twentieth century saw the emergence of Basque and Catalan regionalist parties that broke the hold of caciquismo over local government in their territories. Finally, the Second Republic (1931 – 39), itself ushered in by the defeat of the monarchist parties in the 1931 municipal elections, established a relatively decentralized 'integral state', which allowed regional autonomy for the Catalans and Basques, and greater freedom for local councils (Carr, 1983:603 – 51; Vandelli, 1982: 43 – 55).

The authoritarian dictatorship established after the 1936 – 39 Civil War moved immediately to destroy these decentralized structures.

Regional autonomy in Catalonia and the Basque country was suppressed, and elected local councils were replaced by followers of the National Movement, the new single party of the Francoist regime. A legal and institutional framework for local government was gradually formulated between 1945 and 1955 through a series of legislative acts and decrees (Medhurst, 1973; CEUMT, 1983). Mayors and civil governors were once again appointed by central government, and their political role underlined by their statutory position as local heads of the National Movement. Local councillors were now elected through a complex system of corporatist representation and co-option, based on principles of 'organic democracy', but in practice entirely undemocratic and easily manipulated by the appointed officials. The old techniques of administrative controls and tutelage were revived, and the functions of local councils were eroded further by encroachments of the state field agencies. The financial resources available to the councils were strictly limited. Local government expenditure by the early 1970s amounted to only 10 per cent of total public expenditure and less than 2.5 per cent of gross domestic product (GDP), levels far lower than those found in the rest of West Europe (Uribarri, 1978:56).

The severe social problems created by the accelerated economic development after the 1950s, bringing rapid industrialization, massive rural exodus, high levels of urban growth and increasing regional disparities, contributed to a rising demand for new public services and infrastructure in areas such as education, health, transport, housing and social welfare. Neither the heavily fragmented and weakly financed local councils nor the unco-ordinated efforts of the sectoral field services of central government were able to provide these new elements. Deficits in essential services were especially acute in the burgeoning metropolitan areas of Madrid, Barcelona and Bilbao, and complicated by the anarchy resulting from lax and deficient urban planning mechanisms that catered almost wholly to the needs of private development (Wynn, 1984). Failure to make provision for schools, hospitals, parks, environmental protection or even the basic rudiments of paved streets, sewerage and an adequate water supply, tended to undermine the legitimacy of public authorities, especially local government. The early 1970s saw the rise of highly organized protest movements in many of the large towns, mobilized around urban issues (Castells, 1984; Borja, 1977). These movements, with those of students, trades unionists and regionalists, contributed greatly to the pressures for political change, and formulated demands for both the restoration of democracy and a thorough decentralization of the state.

With the transition to democracy and the adoption of a new constitution in 1978, it was widely expected that the deficiencies and weaknesses of local government would soon be rectified (Uribarri, 1978). However, the awaited reforms were slow in arriving, and even by 1985, some crucial issues had still not been resolved.

The treatment of local government in the 1978 Constitution is relatively brief, involving only four of twenty-two articles in Title VIII (arts 137–58), 'On the Territorial Organization of the State', most of the others being devoted to the new regions. On the matter of the provinces and municipalities, the constitution offers guarantees for their autonomy, allows the creation of intermunicipal bodies and sets out a very broad outline for local finances. The articles dealing with regional autonomy are far more detailed. The new regions are endowed with legislative and executive powers over a wide range of areas, including housing, urban and regional planning, agriculture, transport, health, education, social welfare and culture, according to the terms of their individual autonomy statutes. They are also granted responsibility for local government affairs in general, within the framework set out in 'basic' national legislation. At present, after a long and arduous process of negotiation seventeen autonomous regions have been created, covering the entire Spanish territory, each with its own directly elected government. While the devolution of functions and personnel from the central government has not yet been completed, and some aspects of the financial arrangements remain to be determined, the appearance of the regions marks a clear break with the centralizing traditions of the state, and a move towards a quasi-federal system. The Spanish term for these arrangements is *Estado de las Autonomias* — State of the Autonomies.

The local elections of April 1979 resulted in victories for the left-wing opposition in most large towns, with coalitions of *Partido Socialista Obrero Español* (PSOE — Socialist), *Partido Comunista de España* (PCE — Communist) and smaller parties controlling 1800 of 8000 municipalities, containing 70 per cent of the population. The situation facing the newly elected municipal and provincial councillors was difficult in many respects. The transitional period following Franco's death, with local government continuing under appointed officials, was a lengthy one and many of the features of the Franco regime persisted. Moreover, a number of municipal councils in the larger cities were heavily in debt and their internal organization in a state of chaos. The new democratic councillors had difficulties in obtaining information about the real state of finances or even the number of officials employed by the council. Instead of meeting the demands of local residents for improved services and increased levels of spending, many councils have had to direct their efforts towards implementing austerity programmes and rationalizing their administration.

However, legislative and financial reforms were obstructed for several years by the failure of the minority *Union del Centro*

Democratico (UCD — Centrist) government in Madrid to reach agreement with either the Socialists or the regionalists on the issue of local government. Consequently, UCD resorted to a series of 'urgent measures', usually in the form of decrees or decree-laws. These removed the most blatant restrictions on the activities of local government and provided some new financial resources for the hard-pressed councils, but fell short of the global solutions required (CEUMT, 1981:5–10).

The PSOE government that came to power in the general election of October 1982 made a commitment to secure the legal and financial autonomy of local government through structural reform. Its progress has been slowed by the equally pressing need to control public expenditure and to seek a lasting consensus on local government issues with the opposition parties, including both the conservative *Coalicion Popular* (CP) and the Basque and Catalan nationalists, *Partido Nacionalista Vasco* (PNV) and *Convergencia i Unio* (CiU). A new Local Government Act (*Ley de Bases de Regimen Local* — LBRL) was passed by Parliament in March 1985. Meanwhile, the position of the Socialists at the local level has been bolstered by their gains in the May 1983 local elections giving them sole control over 2640 municipal councils (including thirty-nine of the fifty towns with more than 100,000 residents), and thirty-five of the forty-three provincial councils.

The 1985 Local Government Act (LBRL) specifies only the general principles regarding the territory, internal organization and functions of local government, leaving it to future regional legislation to determine the more concrete details. The question of the provincial councils' role proved to be a particular source of controversy during negotiations over the LBRL, and their status tends to vary according to the region within which they are located. In some cases, new single-province regional governments have been formed, absorbing all of the functions, personnel and facilities of the previous provincial councils, alongside others granted in their autonomy statutes. The situations in the other, multi-provincial regions provide a number of differing models. The Catalan nationalists have been hostile in principle to the continued existence of the four provincial councils in Catalonia, seen as artificial devices imposed by Madrid to divide and weaken the region. They have sought instead to restore a more traditional territorial division of Catalonia into thirty-six *comarcas* or districts, as a basis both for local self-government and new regional field services. The Catalan regional government, or *Generalitat*, in 1980 passed a bill to abolish the provincial councils as a first step towards recreating the comarcas, but this was ruled out by the Constitutional Court (Vandelli, 1982:360–7). The nationalists, nevertheless, remain determined to allow the councils as few powers as possible. In contrast, the Basque nationalists, who remain deeply attached to the historical traditions and rights of their three component provinces, Alava, Guipuzcoa and Viscaya, have tended to strengthen the powers and functions of the provincial councils, even at the expense of the new regional government. Elsewhere, the central government, under UCD and later PSOE, has worked to set up more co-operative arrangements, whereby most of the regions' executive functions would be carried out by the provincial councils, under supervision from the regional government. This was seen as a means of avoiding costly duplication of functions and the proliferation of overlapping and competing bureaucracies between the provincial and regional levels.

The LBRL attempts to reconcile all of these perspectives, maintaining the existence of the provinces, but giving the regions considerable leeway to define their powers and to set up alternative units of local government such as the comarcas. It also allows for the creation of new bodies for the metropolitan areas, and for other types of voluntary joint boards to be set up by the local councils themselves. In the large municipalities, internal decentralization is possible through the formation of neighbourhood district councils. Several large municipal councils, such as Barcelona and Madrid, have already put into effect schemes of this nature. The new Local Government Act thus introduces more flexibility into the system, breaking radically with the uniformity imposed by traditional arrangements. These structures will permit some councils to overcome problems arising from the survival of large numbers of municipalities with small populations — 4768 out of the 8022 municipalities still have fewer than 1000 inhabitants. But they may also result in added financial and administrative burdens by multiplying the number of government tiers involved in the provision of services (up to six — central government, region, province, comarca, municipality and neighbourhood district; see Figure 1).

Turning to the internal organization of local government, the LBRL generally strengthens the powers of the mayor at the expense of the council as a whole. The mayor is empowered for the first time to appoint an executive committee composed solely of the parties forming the majority within the council, in contrast to the previous practice of having a 'permanent committee' with proportional representation of all parties. The plenum of the council does retain some power to keep the mayor in check, notably through a vote of censure to remove him or her in favour of an alternative candidate.

The 1985 Local Government Act has provided answers to some of the important questions regarding the future shape of the lower tier of government that have been pending since the beginning of the transition to democracy. Those issues that remain will be determined in the promised Local Finance Bill, in the forthcoming legislation of the individual regional governments, and through the actual practice of local councils themselves as they develop over the years.

The importance of local government
Local government in Spain has had a relatively small role, in comparison with other West European states. Under the traditional administrative system, it remained subordinate to central government, carried out few functions and was increasingly marginalized over a long period. During the transition to democracy, despite the severe problems of local authorities both in delivering services and in preserving their own legitimacy with the population, the required reforms were given a

FIGURE 1
Spain: territorial structures of local government

Traditional System

CENTRAL GOVERNMENT

PROVINCIAL COUNCILS (50)

Metropolitan Corporation
(Barcelona only)

Joint Boards

MUNICIPAL COUNCILS (8022)

New System (Local Government Act 1985)

CENTRAL GOVERNMENT

REGIONAL GOVERNMENTS   REGIONAL GOVERNMENTS
(Single-province) (7)   (Multi-province) (10)

PROVINCIAL COUNCILS (43)

Comarcas or Intermediate Level Units
(to be created by Regional Govts.)

Metropolitan Authorities

Joint Boards

MUNICIPAL COUNCILS (8022)

Neighbourhood Districts

low priority compared with other, admittedly pressing, political issues.

Local government expenditure as a proportion of GDP in 1985 remained extremely small by West European standards (4.7 per cent), but had doubled since 1973 (2.2 per cent) within a public sector that had also been expanding rapidly (from 23.0 per cent to 40.3 per cent of GDP). Local government's share of public expenditure itself actually declined over the first half of this period, from 9.5 per cent in 1973 to 9.1 per cent in 1979, when the first democratic local councils were created. Its share has since increased slightly, to around 12 per cent. This modest rise, however, is overshadowed by the rapid increase in the share of public spending taken by the regional governments as the devolution process has proceeded; from 0.8 per cent in 1979 to 13.5 per tent in 1985. The combined share for local and regional spending (25 per cent) still remains far from the 50 per cent target set in 1981 by an official commission of experts on the devolution process (*Comision de Expertos*, 1982). At present, with the greater concern for austerity shown by the Socialist government, it appears that this goal will not in fact be reached.

A similar picture of the limited nature of local government's role emerges from the manpower figures, according to which in 1984 local government employed 12.9 per cent of public employees, regional government 11.5 per cent, other agencies such as social security 31.1 per cent and central government 44.5 per cent.

The functions of local government
The limited role of local government in public service provision may appear surprising since traditionally, up to the end of the Franco regime, the functions of local councils have usually been formally defined in very broad terms, including 'all matters relating to local interests'. The 1955 Local Government Act contained a long enumeration of functions and services that councils are empowered to undertake (art.101). Nevertheless, the period to 1975 witnessed a steady erosion of local government functions. Sectoral legislation often failed to specify any local government role, or asserted direct controls over previously traditional local functions. Areas such as housing, health and social welfare were largely taken over by the field agencies of the central government. One particular technique associated with these usurpations was the creation of *Juntas*, ad hoc bodies of civil servants from the field and co-opted local representatives, at either the municipal or provincial level, used to bypass the local councils (Medhurst, 1973:189–90). In other cases, lack of technical expertise or finance prevented functions granted by law from being effectively performed by local authorities.

There were wide variations in the outputs of municipalities because of differences in their capacity in these respects. In addition, many services such as public transport, waste collection and disposal, and even sports and cultural amenities, were actually delivered by private contractors rather than the councils themselves. Table 1 identifies the principal functions of a fairly large municipal council (with a population of more than 50,000) and the provincial councils, distinguishing between major (but not necessarily predominant) and minor functions in relation to central government. Tables 2 and 3 analyse local government investment spending by function. These figures may overestimate the role played by local government, as they include public works actually carried out by the state field services, but charged to local councils.

TABLE 1
Spain: local government functions

Function	Municipal councils	Provincial councils
Education	m[1]	m
Health	m	M
Social services	m	m[2]
Housing	m	—
Public transport	M	—
Roads	m	m
Environmental services[3]	M	—
Police	m	—
Fire	M	m
Public markets	M	—
Culture	m	—

M = major function
m = minor function
Notes:
[1]Construction and maintenance of state primary and secondary schools
[2]Orphanages and old people's homes
[3]Parks, cemeteries, water supply, sewerage, waste collection and disposal, and town planning.
Source: Based on CEUMT, *Manual de Formacion Municipal*, 2nd edn, Barcelona: CEUMT, 1983.

The marginal role of local government in most areas is quite apparent. Municipal councils have been largely restricted to the provision of basic environmental services, fire prevention, public markets and local public transport. The provincial bodies, at the end of the Franco era, were reduced to managing a few hospitals, old people's homes, orphanages and asylums, and the provincial road network.

Local government practice since the transition has been more expansionary in nature, as municipalities have developed new services in the

TABLE 2

Spain: share of central and local government in public investment expenditure
by function, 1973–77
(Per cent)

Function	Central government	Local government
Education/culture	81.8	18.2
Health and social services	82.2	17.8
Housing	95.7	4.3
Environmental services	35.2	64.8
Transport/highways	89.7	10.3
Agriculture	98.7	1.3
Other	96.2	3.8

Source: X. Russines and P. Galdon, 'Inversion y Haciendas Locales', *Informacion Comercial Española*, May 1979.

TABLE 3

Spain: distribution of local government capital expenditure by function,
1973–77

Function	Municipal councils Pop. > 50,000	Municipal councils Pop. < 50,000	Provincial councils[1]	Total
Education/culture	9.8	13.8	6.8	9.3
Health/social services	1.0	2.3	14.1	6.7
Housing	0.8	2.4	1.2	1.3
Environmental services	46.7	43.0	34.3	40.9
Highways	19.9	22.1	32.6	25.7
Public services/ economic aid	2.9	5.1	2.0	3.0
Other	18.5	11.2	6.9	12.2
Total	100.0	100.0	100.0	100.0

[1]Including investment grants to small municipalities.
Source: X. Russines and P. Galdon, 'Inversion y Haciendas Locales', *Informacion Comercial Española*, May 1979.

areas of culture, education, health and social welfare, and increased their role in town planning and in the building of urban infrastructure, insofar as finances and the existing legal framework have allowed. Many councils have also taken into municipal ownership services previously contracted from private operators, such as bus services and waste disposal, often because they were making huge losses.

The Local Government Act of 1985 contains a long section devoted to the functions of local councils. As in previous legislation, it begins with a general definition of competence: 'The Municipality, in the furtherance of its interests and within the scope of its powers can promote all types of activity and provide those public services which contribute to satisfying the needs and aspirations of the local community' (art.24, clause 1). But it also provides a new comprehensive list of the municipal council's functions (art.24, clause 2), which include some responsibilities in fields such as public security, passenger transport and traffic management, public health and consumer protection, housing and town planning, leisure and cultural amenities, building regulations, social services and school building. The municipal councils may carry out other functions delegated to them by the central government or the regions, under supervision. They are also permitted to provide complementary services to those of the other levels in the areas of education, culture, housing, health and environmental protection.

The functions of the provincial councils were defined with far less precision, thanks to the controversies over their role, discussed above. The Act appears to allow as much leeway as possible for each region to determine the future content of its provincial councils' activities, but calls for the co-ordination of municipal services in order to guarantee an integrated, adequate provision throughout the provincial territory; juridical, economic and technical assistance, and co-operation with municipal councils, especially those with fewer resources and less management capacity; the provision of public services of an intermunicipal character, and in general, the promotion and administration of the particular interests of the province. The only activity of the provincial councils delineated by the Act with any specificity concerns the approval of an annual investment plan (*Plan Provincial de Obras y Servicios*), to cover some of the needs of smaller municipalities within the province, funded jointly by the provincial council, the regions and central government. As in the case of the municipal councils, the provincial council can also take on those functions delegated to it by the regional or central government.

Article 80 of the Act grants both levels of local government a general power to carry out economic activities. They are also permitted to create public monopolies within their territory concerning specified services, above all utilities and transport undertakings, subject to approval from the regional government.

Most of the functions designated by the Act as belonging to local government are by no means exclusive to the local level, but will in fact be shared with the national and, to an increasing extent, the regional authorities. The Act tries to ensure that future legislation and regulations produced by the central or regional governments will allow local councils to play as full a role as possible. Until these future norms are formulated, and new working relations are established between the different levels of the state, the position of the local councils regarding their functions will remain uncertain.

Discretion

While in theory general definitions of competence should provide the widest of freedoms, in practice they have failed to preserve a set of core functions for local government that are reasonably secure from excessive interference from above. At first sight, the LBRL of 1985 appears to share this same defect. Local councils are endowed with a considerable range of functions, but the actual division of labour will only be clarified by future decisions made by the upper tiers. Under the present system, however, local bodies do at least enjoy the protection of the guarantees concerning their autonomy written into the Constitution. This should permit them, at least in some cases, to challenge legislation by the higher authorities that infringes their rights. By giving the councils recourse to the Constitutional Court, the LBRL has greatly improved the possibility of their mounting a successful defence of their functional role.

Successive local government laws have also tended to include lists of 'minimum service obligations', or mandatory functions. Under the 1955 Act, for example, all municipalities were to provide for things such as rural watchmen; drinking water in outdoor public fountains; street lighting, paving and cleansing; cemeteries, and waste collection and disposal. Towns with a population of more than 5000 were also required to maintain domestic water supply; sewerage; public baths, and a fire service. Among other things, the LBRL of 1985 updated these lists with additional obligations such as the provision of public transport in the largest towns (50,000-plus inhabitants) and of public libraries in towns with more than 5000 inhabitants.

Despite the very basic standard implied by the nature of these items, many of the small localities are likely to be deficient in one or more of them. Such failures to deliver obligatory services in the past merely provided the pretext for greater intervention by the state field services, rather than encouraging efforts to strengthen the capacity of the weaker municipalities.

Up to the present, administrative controls have been concentrated within a general advisory system, although separate sets of norms for technical services and local finances also exist. The general system involved in particular the civil governor in charge of the administration of the provinces, as well as the inspectorate of the Ministry of the Interior. It covered almost the entire range of administrative acts and decisions produced by the local councils, and was backed by a powerful array of potential sanctions. Both civil governors and mayors could suspend any council decisions that they believed were illegal or constituted a threat to 'public order'. Many categories of local acts involved the tutelage of the civil governor or central ministry: the disposal of some kinds of council property, the creation of any new municipal services, contracts for public works or supplies above a given size, subsidies to local organizations and even the naming of streets. The capacity of central government to scrutinize closely the operations of local councils was greatly enhanced by the creation in 1924 of three national corps of town secretaries, auditors and treasurers (*Secretarios, Interventores* and *Depositorios*). These top local government officials were entirely recruited, trained and despatched to their posts by the Ministry of the Interior. They were legally bound to report to the civil governor any signs of irregularities within their local councils. The system of supervision, however, usually operated in a somewhat lax fashion (at least to the point of allowing widespread corruption), relying more on dissuasion than active intervention to keep councils in line. Its overall effect was to encourage immobilism and inhibit local initiatives. In case of determined resistance, the civil governor had the reserve power to dissolve councils and dismiss individual councillors.

With the return to democracy and growing popular pressure for decentralization, it was widely expected that the awaited local government reform would dismantle this oppressive system of controls. In order to appease the most immediate demands of this kind, the UCD government issued its series of 'urgent measures' from 1978 on, which removed many of the existing techniques of control and tutelage. The power to suspend local government acts in particular was completely modified. The civil governor could henceforth challenge these acts only on grounds of illegality, referring them to the administrative courts. Suspension of council decisions could occur only in cases where a clear national interest was at risk, whereupon the court would have to reach a verdict within thirty days. These changes have already greatly attenuated the administrative restrictions on the activities of local councils. Responsibility for administrative supervision, moreover, is increasingly passing into the hands of the regional governments, although the agents of central government can still intervene when national interests are felt to be at stake.

The Local Government Act or LBRL of 1985 drawn up by the PSOE government has further liberalized administrative relations. These are now mainly conceived in terms of co-ordination and collaboration among the various levels. Both the central and regional governments, however, continue to supervise the legality of local government acts, and can demand information concerning all aspects of the councils' activities. Decisions can still be suspended by the representative of central government in the region (*Delegado del Gobierno*, a recently created official roughly equivalent to the regional *prefet* in France), in the event that they entail 'grievous harm for non-local interests' (art.52). Central government, with approval from the Senate, can invoke even more drastic reserve powers and dissolve local councils for the most serious abuses. The Act requires local councils to seek prior approval from the regional government in some cases, such as the creation of local monopoly services. The region also intervenes in conflicts among local authorities. Lastly, the LBRL provides for the break-up of the national corps of local government officials. Officials occupying the posts of secretary, auditor and treasurer will still require national accreditation, but local councillors can now participate in their selection, with central government reserving the right to make the final appointment.

One key factor that continues to hinder local councils in their decisions is the state of local government finances. The penury from which Spanish councils suffer goes far in explaining their limited capacity to provide adequate services. The local fiscal system inherited from the dictatorship remains archaic and unmanageable, including a large number of taxes and fees with high administrative costs and tiny revenues. Income failed to keep pace with inflation, while local authorities were powerless to adjust their tax rates or the composition of tax ordinances. Table 4 shows the various sources of municipal income for 1982. Two of the most important municipal taxes, an urban property tax (*Contribucion Territorial Urbana*) and a business tax (*Licencia Fiscal*) were in fact collected for the councils by central government agencies, which had little incentive to improve revenues through revisions of property values or reform procedures. Other municipal taxes include levies on motor vehicles, land benefit, publicity and luxury goods. The municipal councils also receive a percentage of all national tax income (excluding those taxes already earmarked to be ceded to the regions) as a non-conditional block grant (after 1977 known as the *Fondo Nacional de Cooperacion Municipal* — FNCM). This source accounts for between 30 and 35 per cent of municipal income. Until 1983, no attempt was made to distribute this grant among the councils according to either their fiscal potential or the level of social need; it was allocated on the basis of population size alone, with the larger municipalities receiving larger per capita grants. The provincial councils depend for much of their revenue on a surcharge levied on a state tax, the *Impuesto sobre trafico de Empresas*, a rather crude version of value-added tax (VAT), as well as their own block grant from the central government.

Until 1981 investment budgets were drawn up by the councils on an ad hoc, pluriannual basis, and financed from savings on current

TABLE 4
Spain: municipal council revenue, 1982
(billion Ptas)

Gross revenue	Amount	% of total
Indirect taxes	37.7	5.7
Direct taxes	151.2	23.0
Charges, fees, etc.	154.3	23.5
Grants	219.9	33.5
Loans	70.6	10.8
Other income	23.4	3.6
Total	657.3	100.0

Source: CAMBIO 16, 14 November 1983.

account, 'special contributions' (capital levies on residents and property owners adjudged by the council to benefit directly from the creation of new services or infrastructure), borrowing from both public and private institutions, and state capital grants. Grants for capital investment from central government are relatively scarce, constituting less than 10 per cent of total grants, and are usually subject to special conditions. The smaller municipalities also receive special investment aid from the provincial councils.

The Ministry of Finance has exercised its own particular form of tutelage over local finances. All budgets, tax ordinances and borrowing requests require its prior approval, and may end up heavily modified by it. The council's tax ordinances may also be challenged by local residents in a special court, the *Tribunal Economico-Administrativo*.

Fiscal stress within local councils worsened sharply after Franco's death, in a context of high inflation and lower income growth, and exacerbated by the failure of the undemocratic local authorities before 1979 to contain costs. Municipal councils in all the larger cities began to develop growing current deficits, in which the operating losses of public transport services played an important part. The need to borrow to cover these shortfalls in turn curbed the capacity of these authorities to invest, at a point when public demand for new services and infrastructure was acute.

After the local elections of April 1979, the municipal councils, both individually and later through a new national local government organization, the *Federacion Española de Municipios y Provincias* (FEMP), began to lobby the UCD government to provide greater financial relief through transfers of national resources. Concessions in this area, as in others, took the form of partial short-term measures rather than an overhaul of the finance system. The municipalities were allowed to refinance their accumulated deficits up to the end of 1979 through cheap, long-term credits, with the national budget absorbing 50 per cent of the annual financial charges. The local taxes were given new maximum rates, and some of the Finance Ministry's controls on tax ordinances were relaxed. Consortia of local councils and the central administration were formed to begin the long-delayed (since 1969) task of revising property values as a means of boosting tax revenues. Tax exemptions for state-aided housing (decided by central government, but penalizing local government revenues) were drastically reduced. Finally, the level of municipal participation in national tax receipts through the FNCM was increased from 2 to 7 per cent between 1979 and 1982, an annual rate of increase of 22 per cent in real terms. This series of financial 'urgent measures', while allowing for an expansion in local government spending in the 1980s, does not appear to have kept up with social demand for services, or to have solved the local fiscal crisis. Accumulated deficits on the large municipalities' current accounts reached Ptas 144,000 million (around £750m.) by the end of 1982, with 80 per cent concentrated in four major cities (Barcelona, Madrid, Seville and Valencia), and 40 per cent attributable to public transport.

The PSOE government that came to power in autumn 1982 had promised a far-reaching reform that would guarantee financial autonomy to the local councils, with more streamlined, buoyant local taxes, and a greater share (up to 12 per cent) of national taxation. But the need for financial austerity and the problems caused both by the economic crisis and the costs arising from the regional devolution process have delayed this global reform. Because of the pressures on central government to cut the public spending deficit, the FNCM's share in national taxation, after increasing to 8 per cent in 1983, fell to 6.5 per cent in 1985. The fund has been given a rather greater redistributive role by taking into account the economic and social characteristics of municipalities as well as population. The central government also agreed to absorb the accumulated deficits of the large city councils, but only in return for their submission to a thorough audit by the Finance Ministry and controls on their spending over the next three years, including a freeze on hiring. On the other hand, discretion over local government finances has increased in a number of ways. In 1984, local authorities were granted complete freedom to vary the rates of the urban property tax and to impose a new, optional income tax surcharge (without limit) on residents. The LBRL in 1985 removed local taxation from the jurisdiction of the special tax courts, and empowered councils to take full control over the collection of the urban property and business taxes.

At first sight, one would expect these innovations to be welcomed by local councillors as a major addition to their resources and an enhancement of their capacity to manage their own affairs. But the introduction of the income tax surcharge, coming on top of several years of steady growth in national taxation, has proved particularly unpopular with councillors and residents alike, and has led to mass demonstrations and a series of challenges in the administrative courts. Councils have been forced to suspend or rescind their decisions to make use of the surcharge. Many of the smaller municipalities are also reluctant to take over the task of tax collection because of inadequate administrative capacity. Meanwhile, the national organization FEMP has continued to press for a fundamental restructuring of local taxation; an increase in the level of block grant, and the creation of new funds for municipalities at the regional level. The Local Finance Bill promised by central government may fulfil some of these demands.

Since 1979, local government discretion has been significantly enhanced through the protection of its status afforded by the new constitution, the elimination of many of the previous forms of administrative control, and the provision of new financial resources. But as the recent developments in the area of local government finance demonstrate, new formal rights and resources can mean greater political pressure on local authorities. While controls by central government may have been loosened, the constraints imposed on local government by its political and economic environment appear to have reduced its room for manoeuvre overall.

Access of local elites to the centre
Local government in Spain has enjoyed limited discretion in delivering a narrow range of services, although both have expanded during the transition to democracy. What is the capacity of local authorities and elites to influence political processes in central government, either to increase their own autonomy, or to win advantages for their own areas in the distribution of financial resources and other policy benefits? Access to the centre, through formal or informal channels for communication and negotiation, could in some circumstances be a means of compensating for the limited scope and freedom of local government.

It is difficult to evaluate the degree of access that existed under the Francoist regime, in the absence of democratic mechanisms of political representation. At first sight, the formal political weight of local councillors at the national level might appear to have been considerable. Within the national *Cortes* (Parliament), the indirectly elected representatives of local councillors comprised 111 of a total 573 members. The significance of this representation was minimized, however, through the manipulation of the electoral process by the regime, and the submissive attitude of the Francoist parliament to the dictatorship. Moreover, insofar as local authorities themselves were the appointed or co-opted creatures of central government, they were not a legitimate reflection of local interests. Other official channels, through the administrative hierarchy of mayors, civil governors and Interior Ministry, or via the field services of individual departments, were also largely unsuited to the expression of local demands, since all of these agents depended entirely on the confidence of their superiors, rather than local support. This system served to suppress and contain local discontent, rather than to provide redress. In the face of more persistent protest, the most frequent response by central government was the replacement of individual officials.

The blockage of access through formal political and administrative mechanisms meant that local authorities tended to resort to informal contacts with important figures at the centre, thus creating sets of clientelistic networks. As Medhurst (1973) suggests: 'Instead of channelling demands through Governors, authorities frequently preferred to approach leading bureaucrats, businessmen, military commanders and even churchmen possessing direct access to the national political elite.' While this form of access was inadequate for the purpose of bargaining over the general rights and needs of local government, it did allow some authorities to influence the distribution of public funds by the centre and meet their most pressing problems. In many cases, however, clientelism led to the misallocation of resources or simply lapsed into corrupt practice. In general, the restricted nature of access increased the weakness and dependence of local government under Francoism and aggravated the frustrations felt by local elites towards the end of the regime, especially when these coincided with regionalist aspirations.

The transition to democracy after 1975 has opened up several new avenues of contact between the centre and locality. The need to establish a firm consensus as a basis for the new democratic institutions has greatly increased the importance of bargaining processes among the various political forces; this was especially apparent in the course of regional devolution, during which regional elites directly negotiated with central government over the terms of their autonomy statutes, and subsequent transfers of services and resources. The new status of local government within the democratic regime has been the subject of similar negotiations. To some extent, this process has continued to depend on informal, face-to-face encounters between key figures at the local and national levels, but it is gradually becoming more structured around the political parties and other formal institutions.

The new democratic political parties and their elected representatives at various levels of the state now provide one of the chief means of access for local authorities to the centre. This development has been encouraged by the impact of the electoral system of proportional representation with fixed lists, which has tended to marginalize independent candidates from elected posts at all levels. Incompatibility laws limit the possibilities for a *cumul des mandats*, by prohibiting elected members from holding more than one full-time post within the public sector. However, some local councillors have become national political figures. This is particularly evident in the case of PSOE, which built up local strongholds before winning power in Madrid in 1982. Four of the fourteen ministers in the present Socialist government have had previous experience in local or regional government. The senate also has a modest 'federal' element in its composition, in that the regional assemblies appoint a small number of representatives (one each, plus one for every one million inhabitants of their region), in addition to 208 directly elected senators from provincial constituencies.

The internal organization and relationships between local party units and their national leadership vary considerably among the different parties. All the major parties have adopted federal structures that match the regional institutions created since 1979, and regional divisions within parties have become increasingly salient in recent years. The main parties of the centre and right, UCD (now defunct), AP and PDP, appear to have absorbed many of the clientelistic networks and agents that existed under Franco, and these now operate within the context of democratic politics. The formation of autonomous regional governments has vastly expanded the possibilities for distributing political patronage. In some cases, this has meant that regional funding available to local councils has been directed almost exclusively to councils controlled by certain parties, excluding the opposition. The president of the regional government or a leading national deputy from a province usually plays a key role in these networks, uniting groups of local elected officials around them.

The parties of the Left, PSOE and PCE, while by no means immune from clientelism, are more clearly defined in ideological terms, and the discipline exerted by central party apparatuses appears rather stronger. Local councillors play an important role within these parties, and local government issues are prominent within national party programmes and agenda. Following its gains in the May 1983 elections, PSOE has more than 28,000 municipal councillors, 16 per cent of its total membership. The influence of this 'municipal lobby' in policy terms, however, is less clear-cut than its numerical strength suggests, and must be balanced against other important interests within the party, notably those of the trades unionists in the Socialist affiliate, *Union General de Trabajadores* (UGT), as well as the national political and economic strategies pursued since 1982 by the Socialist central government, which have often tended to run counter to commitments made to the needs of local government.

Finally, the Basque and Catalan nationalist parties, PNV and CiU, present a third form of articulating local interests at the centre, as part of the package of regional demands that the Basque and Catalan governments and nationalist representatives in parliament attempt to negotiate with the central government in Madrid. The specific interests of local authorities are particularly well represented within PNV, which has sought to strengthen the 'historic rights' of the three provincial councils and the municipalities (the vast majority of which it controls), at times even at the expense of the Basque regional government. Within CiU, power appears to be concentrated more in the hands of a regional elite (that is, members of the regional government and the CiU national deputies) than the party's local councillors, especially since the latter have failed to gain control of any of the large town councils. In order to strengthen their influence at the centre, the Catalan nationalists have played a leading role in the formation of a new party, *Partido Reformista Democratico* (PRD), made up of regionalists and other small groups in the rest of Spain. In alliance with CiU, PRD could challenge the Socialists in future general elections.

The local authorities have also devised an independent means of expressing their specific interests, through local government associations. The most important of these is FEMP, established in 1981 by the mayors of the largest cities. More than 4000 of the 8000 municipalities are now members. Although these include councils controlled by Communists and Conservatives, FEMP is to a large extent dominated by the Socialists and in some ways operates as the institutional adjunct of the 'municipal lobby' at work within PSOE. Local councils controlled by the Basque and Catalan nationalists have refused so far to join FEMP and have formed separate organizations. FEMP is now in the process of restructuring itself as a federation of regional associations, which may prove more attractive to the nationalists. Financed by subscriptions from individual councils, it maintains a number of specialized committees, provides seminars and courses for local councillors, and mounts campaigns on local government issues.

The most important of FEMP's activities consists of negotiating on behalf of local councils with central government. In recent years, it has played a crucial role in a number of key decisions. It was consulted at several stages concerning the LBRL passed in 1985, and won significant concessions on issues such as the internal organization and powers of local councils. FEMP has also been able to influence central government decisions on the level and distribution of grants to local authorities, as was demonstrated in 1985, in the process of fixing budgetary allocations to FNCM. The councils represented within FEMP were able to come to a compromise on the distribution of these funds among themselves. The large city councils agreed to a cut in their own shares relative to the smaller municipalities, in return for special aid from central government for the metropolitan areas and for public transport services. This package was subsequently adopted by the Ministry of Finance and by Parliament, although they reduced the total level of grant proposed by FEMP. Even in this case, however, the continuing importance of face-to-face bargaining and party links was emphasized by the role played by the mayors of Madrid and Barcelona, both influential figures within PSOE, in direct discussions with the Socialist Finance Minister, Miguel Boyer, to persuade him to accept FEMP's proposals. FEMP's position as the official representative of local vis-a-vis central government has been made statutory through the 1985 Local Government Act, with the creation of a consultative joint commission, the *Comision de Colaboracion del Estado con las Corporaciones Locales*, whose members are appointed in equal numbers by central government and FEMP. The commission is empowered to make recommendations on all matters relating to local government, and to appeal to the Constitutional Court to arbitrate in conflicts between central and local government.

The influence of other groups, such as local government officials, the field agencies of central and regional governments, and the professions, on central – local relations and policy making in specific areas is far less clear. There is some evidence that their role in mediating between the central and local levels may have diminished in recent years, compared with that of the elected members and political parties. In particular, the disbanding of the national corps of top officials in the town halls, entailed by the new LBRL, has been viewed by many observers, including the representatives of these officials themselves, as a significant weakening of their position.

The officials within the various sectoral field agencies of central government, which under the previous regime had become increasingly powerful, have also been affected both by the transfer of many of these agencies to the regions, and by the administrative reforms that have been carried out by central government, especially under the Socialists. The latter have resulted in three major changes: a drastic reduction in the number of specialist corps (from more than 260 to 40); severe limitations on civil servants' practice of accumulating administrative posts or combining these with activities in the private sector, and the strengthening of the powers of the civil governors and the new government delegates at the regional level to co-ordinate the remaining agencies of the central state at the provincial and regional levels. The effect of these changes may be to dislocate existing networks and channels among these officials, through which they have been able to influence the formulation and implementation of policies, and mediate between the central and local levels of the state.

The role of other professional groups involved in the provision of public services, such as doctors, architects and lawyers, usually through traditional 'colleges', and that of public-sector unions is probably less significant in Spain than in other West European countries, although some did become active in the democratic opposition in the final years of the dictatorship. Some professions closely involved with local government, such as town planning, do not even possess their own associations as yet. But the present government is about to introduce new legislation on professional bodies, and it seems likely that their influence, with that of the trades unions, will increase.

Summing up, it appears that the access of local government to national centres of decision making has been widened since the transition to democracy. This change has mainly been to the benefit of elected local councillors and has taken a rather hybrid form involving a variety of channels: informal bargaining, party political links and formal structures such as FEMP. The influence of other actors, such as local government officials and the field agencies, appears to have weakened to some extent, or has only begun to develop. One change in particular that may affect the system of access is the progress of regional devolution. In many policy areas, the regions are destined to become the essential mediators between the localities and the centre, and links with the regional capital may in time become more crucial to local councils than those with Madrid.

Regionalism and local government

The overwhelming importance of regionalism in Spain should be clear from the sections above. Regional identities, built on cultural, ethnic and linguistic cleavages, as well as territorial imbalances in economic development, have been steadily reinforced throughout the past 100 years. The regional question has tended to dominate Spanish politics since 1975, and its solution has been seen as crucial to the stability of the new democratic institutions. Regionalist or nationalist parties are present throughout the country. The Basque and Catalan nationalists in particular have attained a near-hegemonic position, in electoral terms, in their respective regions, and in some ways provide the most formidable opposition to PSOE in the country as a whole. The Socialist Party itself is divided internally along regional lines, as are most other political parties and interest groups (including FEMP).

The institutional structures created by the devolution process, in the form of elected regional governments wielding important legislative and executive powers, are both the result and an added impetus to the regionalist movement in Spain. These bodies will in due course control the bulk of public services (for example, education, health, social

welfare, housing), as well as various other forms of economic intervention. The devolution process itself has been marked by continuing
tensions between the regions and central government, particularly over
the issues of finance and linguistic rights. The Basque and Catalan
nationalists won a significant victory in the defence of the regions'
prerogatives, when the Constitutional Court, in August 1983, ruled
against the 'harmonization' law (*Ley Organica de Armonizacion del
Proceso Autonomico* — LOAPA). This law, supported by both UCD
and PSOE, sought to assert the right of central government to impose
measures on the regions in the interest of uniformity and efficiency.
LOAPA's defeat has provided additional guarantees for regional
autonomy, to the point that some observers see an evolution towards
federalism or even 'confederal' arrangements as inevitable.

To some extent, the position of local government within the
Spanish state is closely linked to that of the regions. The weakness of
local government in the last years of the dictatorship, associated with
critical deficits in urban services and a general loss of legitimacy, was
a major contributory factor to the growth of regionalism. The
widespread aspirations to regional autonomy (or even independence,
in the case of Basque and Catalan nationalists) and the movement for
greater decentralization at the local level are to some extent parallel
and mutually supportive, in that both have sought to dismantle the
traditional mechanisms of centralized authoritarian rule from Madrid
and to bring political power closer to the level of individual citizens
and their local communities. In many regions, the provincial and
municipal councils have played a part in initiating the process of
regional devolution, a role given to them by the Constitution.

Despite areas of affinity, however, the relationship between
regionalism and local government is not exempt from ambiguity and
tension. There are signs of this in the stance of the regionalist parties
themselves. The Basque nationalist PNV, for example, is split between
'regionalists' and 'provincialists'. The president of the Basque
regional government, Garaikoetxea, was forced to resign when the
'provincialists' pushed through a law (*Ley de Territorios Historicos*)
in the Basque parliament to strengthen the three provincial councils
against the region. This dispute was made more acute by the fact that
these provincial rights include important fiscal privileges, which allow
the provinces to collect almost all taxes in the place of central
government (with the latter receiving a negotiable lump sum payment,
the *cupo*, for common services).

There are equally serious problems in Catalonia, where the regional
level is controlled by Catalan nationalists, but most of the provincial
and municipal councils are in the hands of the Socialists. The rivalry
between these two forces has meant some degree of friction between

regional and local governments. The attempt by the nationalists to abolish the provincial councils has already been discussed. The status of the Barcelona metropolitan corporation is also a point of contention, as the nationalists see it as a potential counterweight to their influence in the region. However, as many services within the metropolitan area, such as public transport, roads and hospitals, are provided by both local government and the region, co-ordination is essential.

In the rest of Spain, regional–local relations appear to be more harmonious. But as the devolution process is completed, the influence of the regions on local government is likely to increase. The constitutional position of the regions gives them the right to legislate on matters concerning the boundaries, internal organization and powers of local government, as in most federalist systems. Many individual functions of local government, such as town planning, transport, education, culture, health and social welfare, will tend to be determined by sectoral legislation, again, within the regional domain. Similarly, the administrative and technical supervision, and co-ordination of local councils' activities will in future be carried out to a large extent by the regional executives. While controls by the region are unlikely to be as strict as those exercised by central government in the past, they may become a new source of conflict. Local discretion may also be limited if regional governments decide to set up their own field agencies to provide services in local areas, rather than delegating responsibilities to local authorities (a development that clauses in LOAPA specifically sought to restrict).

The financial role of the regions vis-a-vis local government should also become more pronounced. Present financial arrangements favour the regions far more than local government. In 1985, for example, spending by the regions grew by 28 per cent, compared with 7 per cent for local government. In addition to their own taxation, the regions receive grants from central government to cover the operating costs of services transferred to them and for capital investment. Because of the methodology used in determining these grants, in recent years they have increased in value at a higher rate than inflation (the so-called 'financial effect'). With added resources, the regions may come to replace central government, at least in part, as a source of funding for local councils. Regional governments already provide capital grants to municipalities for individual investment projects, and some experts, including FEMP, have called for the establishment of regional block grants to supplement the national FNCM. While such development promises immediate benefits to hard-pressed local authorities, it may also involve a greater dependency on the regions, especially if it is not accompanied by an adequate reform of local taxation.

The elements outlined above point to ways in which regional

autonomy tends to compete or conflict with decentralization to the level of local government. While both the Constitution and the 1985 Local Government Act do provide legal protection of local autonomy from regional encroachment, the possibilities exist for some form of 'recentralization' at the regional level to emerge in the future. Such an outcome will depend on whether regionalism in Spain maintains its present political momentum, in the face of resistance from both central government above and the local authorities below.

Conclusions

Within the traditional system of territorial administration that existed in Spain up until the 1970s, local government was maintained in a highly subordinate, and even marginal position. Its role within the public sector was strictly limited, and the range of services it provided far narrower than elsewhere in West Europe. Elected local councils were subject to a set of severe administrative controls, weakened by fragmentation and penury, and encroached upon by the field services of central government. In political terms, local government served chiefly as a means of support for a succession of oligarchic regimes and to exclude opponents from power. Under the Francoist dictatorship, it lost even its representative character as a means of expressing the needs of localities.

The traditional system entered its final crisis when confronted with the social costs generated by the accelerated economic expansion and urban growth of the 1950s and 1960s. Unable to meet the population's rising demand for public services, new forms of infrastructure and environmental protection, the legitimacy of local government was undermined in the last years of Francoism, which saw the emergence of a series of protest movements in the large urban areas. These movements in turn contributed to the growing pressure for a return to political democracy and a complete reform of the centralized Spanish state.

Even after the democratic transition, and despite the urgency of the problems faced by local councils, the process of change at the local level has been slow, especially compared with the progress of regional devolution. Local government has continued to be hampered by the restrictive legislation inherited from the previous regime and by the lack of adequate financial resources. Reform has tended to take the form of a series of partial measures that fail to add up to the complete overhaul which is needed. Some improvement has occurred with the arrival of the Socialists in power in central government, and the passage of the 1985 Local Government Act. This legislation has created a more flexible framework for local government, allowing a greater organizational diversity and a broader functional scope for local services, as well as some legal protection for local autonomy. Many of the traditional techniques of administrative control have been abolished or attenuated. The discretion of local government has also been expanded by changes in local government finance, giving local authorities greater control over their own resources and, above all, increasing the overall level of funding. Finally, the access of local government agents to the national centres of decision making has opened up to a considerable extent. Although still dependent to some degree on face-to-face encounters between key figures and clientelistic networks, access is gradually becoming more structured through the emergence of political parties and a national local government organization.

All these developments have had positive effects on local government in terms of its autonomy and influence within the Spanish political system. Nevertheless, there are signs that its position remains precarious in some respects. Many of the measures designed to allow discretion on the part of local authorities appear rather to have increased the pressures on them, in the context of acute economic crisis and a continuing high level of demand for local services. This pressure is particularly evident in the area of finance, and a lasting solution to the problems of local fiscal stress has not yet been devised. At the same time, local autonomy may also come under threat in the near future from a tendency towards 'recentralization' at the regional level, due to the expanding role of the new regional governments that have been created. Although the centralist structures of the Spanish state have been decisively dismantled, local government may thus continue to be the 'poor relation' in the 'State of the Autonomies'.

9

Centre and locality: explaining crossnational variation

Edward C. Page and Michael J. Goldsmith

A part of the constitution?

As has been suggested in the preceding chapters, local government is 'part of the constitution' in the countries covered in this book insofar as being part of the constitution is guaranteed by a reasonably long tradition and some claim to popular support as a worthy institution that should be retained. Yet this raises the question, to use Bagehot's term, of whether local government is a dignified or efficient part of the constitution. While many features of local government's past — the mayoral sash, chain or mace and, in some countries, the office of mayor itself — have moved on to become symbolic parts of the constitution, on the evidence presented here the answer to this question is beyond doubt: local government belongs ubiquitously to the efficient part of the constitution.

The reasons for assigning local government to the 'efficient' part of the constitution vary, however, among our seven countries. In functional terms, it is clear that in some states local government provides a larger portion of public services than in others. One of the distinguishing features of Scandinavian and British local government, in contrast with that in Italy, France and Spain, is that some (but not all) of the most costly public services, including education, health, social transfers, police, housing and roads, are formally the responsibility of local government. While this is also true of some South European States, especially for services, they shared, and continue to share, responsibility for financing and running these services with other public agencies, such as central government ministries and special agencies such as the HLM in France. Furthermore, their involvement in these major fields has often been confined to minor matters such as school building or teachers' housing, or maintaining small rural police services.

In functional terms, local government does more in Britain and Scandinavia, and there developed a stronger division of labour between central and local government, than in the southern countries. Table 1 illustrates the degree to which local authorities do different things by comparing manpower and expenditure figures for the seven states. The communes (until recently the major form of elected government, with direct executive powers, at the subnational level), in

1984 accounted for only a small proportion of public spending and manpower levels in South Europe: 14 and 10 per cent, respectively, for Italy, 12 and 2 per cent for France, and 9 and 10 per cent for Spain.

TABLE 1
West Europe: local government expenditure and manpower, 1984

	Local as % of total public expenditure[1]	Local as % of total public employment
Norway	61	64[2]
Denmark	57	57
Sweden	42	54
Britain	26	38
Italy[3]		
communes	14	10
regions, provinces	7	2
France[3]		
communes	12	10
regions, départements	5	1
Spain		
communes	9	10
provinces and regions	13	14

[1]Capital plus current.
[2]Percentage of central plus local government employees only.
[3]Excludes health, which in both France and Italy has formal links to local and regional government respectively, but is financed and organized outside the local government sector.
Source: calculations derived from OECD and IMF sources and from Rose (1985b).

In the late 1970s, the development of regional and provincial government along the lines of a system of local government, that is, the creation of a regional and provincial level of government responsible to a directly elected assembly, has served to expand the range of functions carried out at the subnational level in the South European countries. So far, these institutions have added only a modest portion of public spending to elected subnational government expenditure in Italy and France (7 and 5 per cent, respectively) and had very limited manpower implications (accounting for 2 and 1 per cent of public-sector manpower in Italy and France, respectively). However, with the recent transfer of further functions to subnational government in France, one would expect figures for manpower and expenditure in the regions and *départements* to increase substantially. The changes have stronger implications in Spain, where the regions and provinces are responsible for 13 per cent of total public spending and 14 per cent of public employment, dwarfing the communes' contribution to public service delivery: on Clegg's evidence, Spain has moved closest to a federal system of our South European cases.

Whether these regional and provincial institutions can or should be equated with local government is an issue that we cannot hope to resolve here. All we can do is to point out that, in the past few years, a significant proportion of what was almost exclusively a central government responsibility in the countries of South Europe has not devolved to the formal sphere of responsibility of subnational government institutions. Moreover, the transfer of functions from the centre to regional and provincial government is likely to increase their importance as service delivery institutions. Even so, the North –South distinction, in terms of functions, still obtains.

The distinctions in terms of discretion are not so simply made. The general constitutional framework of local government does not offer any clear distinction between our seven countries on the basis of whether they have high or low discretion. It has been shown that, in France and Spain, constitutional guarantees of the omnicompetence of local government have little effect on its discretion to deliver services. In these two countries, the absence of a clearly defined set of local services gave rise in the past to continued erosion in the range of local functions, rather than increased freedom for local authorities to choose which services they wished to deliver. Moreover, even where such an erosion has not taken place, as in much of Scandinavia, most of the major services are mandated by central legislation, allowing local discretion about the services to be delivered only in policy areas that are small in both financial and manpower terms. These factors cast doubt on the assumption that the doctrine of ultra vires in Britain really does, in practice, limit local authority discretion in a particularly distinctive way: the choice of which services to deliver does not offer a powerful means for the exercise of local discretion.

Nor do revenue systems offer a key to distinguishing patterns of discretion. Local taxation systems do, of course, vary. However, those in which local revenue is based on buoyant and broad taxes, for example, Norway, are just as susceptible to fiscal limitations as those with limited taxes and no buoyancy, for example, Britain. In all the systems, some form of central limitation exists on the revenue-raising capacity of local government.

It is not possible to come to a general conclusion, even an impressionistic one, about the degree of discretion in service delivery that local authorities have in practice. It appears that the discretion local government has varies from service to service. Moreover, some services seem to attract stronger central regulations and norms than others. It is therefore difficult in practice to distinguish the discretion local government enjoys from the functions it fulfils. Where local government has responsibility for education, for example, it is characteristically heavily regulated in terms of major aspects of service delivery, above all in determining school age. Even where education appears relatively less centrally regulated, as in Britain, the scope for local discretion is bounded by a number of non-statutory national constraints, such as the influence of examination boards on school curriculums. Transfer payments and health services are other functions that appear to attract a high degree of central regulation, whereas services such as culture and leisure facilities, which take a large proportion of the budgets of many Spanish, French and Italian municipalities, are typically constrained by fewer national regulations in all countries.

One cannot reduce discretion to one dimension and suggest that local government in one country has more of it than another. The fact that, for example, local government in France has a high degree of discretion in providing cultural services, and that these account for a large and growing proportion of local spending, might on the one hand be taken as a sign of greater discretion for local government — it is providing the kind of service that attracts comparatively few regulations, in contrast to others, such as education and social transfers, which are important services typically provided by Scandinavian local government. On the other hand, the Scandinavian countries probably have just as much discretion in providing cultural services as their French counterparts. In other words, in addition to providing a number of highly regulated functions, local authorities also provide several that are less highly regulated.

It is possible to point to characteristic differences in the way in which discretion is constrained in the northern and southern countries in this study, although this does not of itself say much about differences in the extent of discretion. There are two broad ways in which central government regulates local authorities. First, where involvement in the detailed issues of local decisions is built into the form of regulation (administrative regulation) and, second, where such detailed involvement is minimized (statutory regulation — cf. Kelsen, 1949). From the centre's perspective, statutory regulation is a method of 'remote control'; once the laws have been passed, local authorities can do as they please so long as it is within the law; the only form of central intervention consists of quasi-judicial interpretation (for example, through courts and auditors) of legality. This system contrasts with that based on administrative regulation, in which local government legality is defined through the individual decisions of state officials themselves. In addition, administrative approval of a legally binding nature is often necessary before action can be taken, as well as the judicial post hoc validation found under statutory regulation.

Administrative regulation is far from remote control, since it involves the grant of state approval for local actions on a routine basis and therefore involves central government in the details of local government. Administrative regulation characterized the South European countries even before the changes in the local government system of the past ten years or so; statutory regulation, with relatively little direct involvement by state officials in the details of local decision making, appeared more predominant in Britain and Scandinavia. There is, however, evidence to suggest that the development of regional levels of government in South Europe is altering administrative regulation by making this level the major source of administrative regulation.

Excluding Spain for the moment (because the suppression of democracy under Franco makes more hazardous the identification of longer term trends), patterns of access appear to follow this division between the Scandinavian and British systems, on the one hand, and the South European countries, on the other. In the former, there exist large national interest groups of the local authorities through which routine negotiations are conducted surrounding central–local issues. Moreover, these associations are involved in wage negotiations, representing the local authority employers. While there is some representation of serving and former local councillors in national parliaments, this being most marked in Norway where, in 1984, 83 per cent of MPs had been local councillors at some time, the contributors to this book have emphasized that, in the northern countries, this may generate 'sympathy' and 'understanding' for local points of view, but not as strongly and less directly than that generated by the *cumul des mandats* in France.

In contrast to the pressure group form of access in Scandinavia and Britain is the more direct form of access of local to central elites that obtains in France and Italy. The contrasts between French and Italian central–local patterns of access, at least as they existed until the late 1970s, have been well documented by Tarrow (1977); the importance of these direct forms of access, through political parties in Italy and a form of administrative entrepreneurship in France, of which the cumul des mandats is but one aspect, is beyond doubt. It goes well beyond the 'sympathy' and 'understanding' that might be expected of former councillors in the northern countries. In Italy and France, there are positive benefits, in career terms, for a national politician to represent in the national arena the views, not necessarily of 'local government' in the abstract, but of the specific area that he or she represents. In Italy, local elites make a vital contribution to the national parties through the patronage and financial resources at their disposal. Moreover, the power of national pressure groups in Italy and France derives not only from their ability to amass evidence, offer reasoned argument, provide expert advice and threaten non-compliance when appropriate — the basis of local authority pressure group power in Britain and

Scandinavia — but also from the importance of local actors in the national political system; the leading figures of the local authority associations in France are leading national apolitical figures. Moreover, their representation in the senate serves to reinforce their position, giving them a powerful voice within the legislative process.

It is not altogether clear yet whether Spain conforms with our South European model. Under the *caciquismo* in the late nineteenth and early twentieth centuries, Spain appeared to have an extensive form of local clientelism of the sort that later developed into the more direct form of access that we have seen in France and Italy (Lemarchand and Eisenstadt, 1981). However, the Franco regime served to block any real local influence on the centre. In consequence, as Clegg shows, access tended to take the form of a restricted direct access by local elites to national bureaucrats, businessmen and military officers. The recent reintroduction of democracy makes difficult any assessment of patterns of central–local access. The large associations of local authorities appear to be occupying a central position in central–local bargaining, yet the evidence suggests that, as in France and Italy, the impact of indirect forms of access is bolstered by direct linkages in a way not found in Britain and Scandinavia: party linkages in Spain offer an important means for a particular locality to extract benefits from the centre, and even in the work of the national associations these direct relationships are assuming an importance that further distinguishes the northern from the southern patterns of central–local relations.

To summarize: in the North European countries, by which we mean Britain, Denmark, Norway and Sweden, local government has traditionally had more extensive functions than in the South, including France, Italy and Spain, where local government had responsibility for a narrow range of functions until the end of the 1970s, since when subnational government (but not necessarily the traditional municipalities) has received a number of additional functions. There are no clear differences in the degrees of discretion enjoyed by local authorities in the seven countries: local discretion appears to vary more between services than between states, and it is impossible to state that any one country has a more restrictive regime than another. Local government in the North European countries has more functions that attract more stringent limitations to discretion through conditions regarding matters such as transfer payments to individuals or requirements concerning education provision. However, the types of limitation on discretion in Scandinavia and Britain differ from those in the South European states because there is greater emphasis in the former on specifying through general norms, statutes and regulations criteria that must be observed (statutory regulation); in the latter, many decisions of local authorities involve the intervention of central officials at an earlier stage in the policy process (administrative regulation).

Patterns of access appear at first sight to be similar across all seven of our countries, in the sense that large interest groups representing local government as a whole constitute an important channel for central–local interaction. However, the strength of direct channels of access, based on the importance of local politics and local legitimacy for national careers, encouraging the development of close links between the centre and specific localities through party or bureaucratic channels, distinguishes the South from the North. Because the South has strong direct forms of access in addition to the indirect forms found in the North, and because these direct forms also serve to enhance the impact of the local government associations in the South, we may conclude that local government has much better opportunities to influence central policy making in the South than it does in the North. In South Europe, not only is the voice of local government as a whole heard at the centre, but also that of the individual municipality.

Explaining patterns of central–local relations

It may appear inappropriate to seek to explain patterns of central–local relations at a time when, in many of the countries included in this study, profound changes in these relations are taking place. This, as we hope to show in this section, need not be a handicap. Indeed, contemporary changes may offer clues to the longer-term forces that shape central–local relations. However, we do intend to limit our initial examination of explanations for differences in central–local relations primarily to the patterns that prevailed prior to the late 1970s. One reason for this is that the nature of subsequent changes in central–local relations remains uncertain in some countries, above all in France and Spain. Moreover, theoretical explanations that apply to the period after the late 1970s should also work for the period before. For clues to the causes of differences in central–local relations, it is better to look at a period about which more is known than the present and the immediate future. We can concentrate initially on a period that is not only better documented, but that also produces stronger contrasts in patterns of functional allocation, access and discretion than is likely to be found after the late 1970s.

Many of the theoretical approaches offer relatively little help in understanding why central–local relations in different countries should differ in the ways outlined in this volume. Instead, theories that explain the role of local government in modern political systems tend to lead one to expect crossnational similarities. For example, the 'dual state' thesis associated with Cawson and Saunders (1983) in various forms suggests, broadly speaking, that some types of functions are inherently more likely to be performed by local government irrespective of the particular political system. This thesis can, of course, claim immunity from the charge that there is no such homogeneity in the crossnational allocation of functions by suggesting that the thesis represents an 'ideal type' — a useful heuristic device for identifying deviations from an abstract pattern of relations. However, such a claim still leaves the task of explaining differences in central–local relations, and there appears to be little in the thesis even to suggest the types of factors that might be included in such an explanation. Similar arguments can be levelled against the literature on fiscal federalism (King, 1984), which seeks to define, among other things, the types of functions that should be assigned to local government through formal models of economic rationality, or the Marxist 'local state' argument that suggests that local government is everywhere just a part of a single bourgeois state structure (Cockburn, 1977).

The impact of what may be termed 'culture' provides another explanation for differences in patterns of central–local relations. Culture has been used as an explanatory variable in many cases, notably in Crozier and his colleagues' cultural model of bureaucracy in France and in Fevolden and Sorensen's contribution to this volume. Particular cultural explanations have, of course, their own individual problems. For example, one could argue that their values of territorial equity and local identity are present in all or most polities. Yet there is a broader problem with cultural explanations: they are often residual explanations, to be resorted to only when no other can be found. Thus it is important to look for alternatives to the broad and rather mysterious cultural explanation for differences in central–local relations.

How can we set about explaining differences in central–local government relations? Of course, it is not possible to offer in a concluding chapter to a descriptive study any comprehensive explanation of such differences. Moreover, there is an enormous range of factors that could be explored, from 'cultural' influences on the shape of central–local relations to a great diversity of social, structural and economic influences. However, at least we might expect a comparative analysis to offer some clues as to the type of explanation that is worth pursuing.

The distinction between northern and southern government systems at first appears to offer such a set of clues — discover what the North and the South have in common, and one has a list of possible topics that could be explored in the context of a comparative explanation. One possible candidate for any list of common features would be the experience of a Napoleonic state, which appeared to leave those systems that came under its influence with a set of institutional relationships that survived long after the end of the Code Napoleon, giving rise to a pattern of central–local relations heavily dependent on a system of administrative regulation. Religious differences between North and South could also be included in the list — Archer's (1979, Chapter 3) comparative study of education, including a comparison of Britain and France, suggests that religion played an important part in shaping the formal organization of education administration. The patterns of access of local to central government, based on direct contacts between national and local politicians in the South, may reflect the fact that South European society remained largely agrarian until well after the Second World War. The assumption here is based on the view that the form of clientelism with which these direct patterns may be linked is associated with a rural way of life. One could also include in the list some sort of difference associated with the relatively later development of a welfare state in the South, on the grounds that the type of small-scale, direct-access local government system that characterized local government there, until at least the 1970s, could survive only insofar as the demands for increased public services could be contained. In contrast, the northern countries share a twentieth-century history of social-democratic regimes concerned to promote equality and equity through the development of welfare-state services. Such regimes have chosen, in Scandinavia to a great extent, and less so in Britain, to use local government as the means to deliver such services, and have shown considerable willingness to overcome local opposition when reform and reorganization of the system have been thought necessary to achieve central policy objectives. The presence of nationally based interest organizations representing local government, and of nationally oriented professions has aided this process, yet allowed the locality considerable discretion in deciding service levels, since local authorities have had the necessary technical expertise to develop the services expected of them by the centre.

Our evidence does not allow us to decide between these types of explanation at present. Moreover, how one might explore such hypotheses in the context of a seven-nation study is problematic. We do not have enough cases to enable us to employ even the crudest of correlation techniques, based on the coincidence of national patterns of central–local relations and social, economic, cultural and political characteristics. How might such explanations for differences be explored?

One way might be to identify the origins of the patterns of differentiation and explore the reasons that local government pursues distinctive paths of development. Thus, we might undertake an historical study of the major local government functions found in some North European countries, such as education, roads, housing and health, and explore why these were developed in the context of local government administration in some countries but not in others. What common features of the social, political, economic or cultural functions — if any — can help us to understand why North European countries tended to use local government as a vehicle for service delivery to a greater extent than southern states? Similarly, to explain different patterns of access, we might look for evidence of the causes of differentiation in the circumstances surrounding the initial development of such patterns. It has been suggested that in France the pattern of cumul des mandats emerged in the second half of the nineteenth century — around the same time that patterns of access characteristic of the 'dual polity' emerged (Thoenig, 1980; Bulpitt, 1983). An understanding of the origins of these differential patterns of development could take us further in understanding contemporary differences in central – local relations.

One of the main problems with this otherwise attractive approach is that it is not adequate simply to identify the origins of differentiation, or even the causes of it, in the mists of history. Why such patterns persist is just as important as their origin. This is not so much a criticism of an historical approach, as a suggestion that it is not enough. Such an approach would demand an explanation that refers to a set of broad features of the local government system that persist in the development of systems of government as a whole. Does our evidence so far suggest any clues as to the types of factor that could make up such an explanation?

One possibility can be found in something that we felt, initially, was a red herring in the comparative study of central – local relations: the size of local government. We could understand our contributors wanting to include local government reorganization, or the lack of it, in the country chapters because it was directly connected with the description of the local government system concerned, and also provided case-study material for generalization about central – local relations in that country. It later became apparent that size might be an important intervening variable linking patterns of functional allocation to patterns of supervision, or regulation and access, and as such might help to provide the sort of clue we needed to enhance our understanding of the role of local government in the development of government systems.

The evidence suggests that central government does not like to leave many important functions to small local units. Such a view does not necessarily follow from central perceptions of 'inefficiency' and 'diseconomies of scale' thought to result from small-scale local government; perhaps more important, central political elites believe that a plethora of small local government units is difficult to control and offers too many points at which political adversaries can shape public policy.

The population size of local government units in the Scandinavian countries appears linked to patterns of functional allocation: local government reorganization was perceived as a necessary accompaniment to the expansion of state services, as Sorenson and Fevolden, Lane and Magnusson, and Bogason have shown. In Britain, as in Scandinavia, the larger local government units, that is, the counties and metropolitan districts, were allocated the major functions in the 1972 reforms, as much for control as efficiency reasons (Sharpe, 1978). The decentralization measures in France, Italy and Spain support this hypothesis: reform of the communes has not come about. Decentralization has taken place not by granting more functions to a system of local government dominated by small communes, but rather by expanding the functions of the larger population provinces and regions, which have become similar, if not identical, to local government units through the direct responsibility of the départements' provincial and regional executive to an elected assembly. In a sense, the development of regions and provinces in South Europe can be regarded as analogous to the consolidation and enlargement of local government in northern Europe. Attempts to reform the basic units of local government, the communes, to equip them to carry out major public services that urbanization made increasingly necessary in the postwar period were notoriously unsuccessful in France and Italy, in large part because of the political resilience of local elites. The creation of regions and provinces allows the development of subnational government without confronting local political elites — indeed, it has their support.

None of this is to suggest, in a deterministic way, that the range of services provided is a function of the size of local government units in any particular country. Indeed, one can point to a few cases where the opposite is true, as when local government reorganization in Britain in the 1970s reduced the functions of local government, despite the creation of large local authorities.

Smaller local government units may also tend to produce administrative rather than statutory control: statutory control suggests a faith by central state actors in the competence and willingness of local government to provide services without the direct supervision of state authorities, and this faith may be less strong where local authorities are mostly so small that they cannot afford much by way of a full-time staff, let alone a professional one. The evidence for this comes from the Scandinavian countries, which shifted strongly towards statutory rather than administrative control in the postwar period, following the expansion, consolidation and consequent 'bureaucratization' of local government. It also comes from France, where, under the old system of local government, the cities developed far greater autonomy, in terms of direct intervention by state administrators, and where under the new system the relationship between the regions and départements, on the one hand, and the communes, on the other, retains much of the old system of administrative regulation; conversely, the relationship between the central state, and the regions and départements appears closer to a form of statutory control.

All this might be taken to be another explanation of the sort which, like that afforded by the Napoleonic state, religion or social structure, relies on a possible 'coincidence' that is very hard to substantiate. However, we suggest that it is more than another vaguely interesting coincidence, because the evidence in this book suggests there is a strong case for believing that patterns of functional allocation, size and forms of supervision are related; such a relationship can be demonstrated by observing the way in which local government has developed in our seven countries. Moreover, such a line of argument, which links size to our dimensions of variation, suggests hypotheses that are capable of further empirical investigation. For example, it suggests that in the actual process, say, of centralizing education in France, the small, fragmented local government system was a material factor in removing education from church administration and placing it in the hands of the central state, a suggestion given some initial support in Vaughan and Archer's study (1971:207).

How such a pattern of small local government managed to survive, even to the point where central government in Italy and France has tended to add larger local government units to the system rather than reform it, is linked to patterns of access. As we have noted, direct patterns of access reflect the importance of local politics to national political careers. It is precisely the importance of local politics that has prevented a major reorganization of local government in Italy and France of the sort experienced in Scandinavia and Britain, that is to say, involving the redrawing of the traditional local government boundaries (Kjellberg, 1985).

If these speculations are correct, it implies that one of the key factors in an explanation for differences in central–local relations involves the conditions under which local politics maintains or loses its importance to national politics. According to some models of the development of intergovernmental relations, one change that might be expected is a diminution of the power of local political elites in the national system, on which direct forms of access as well as resistance to local government reorganization is based. This change follows from the development of powerful professional allegiances and networks among diverse functional groups of administrators at central and local level, as well as the emergence of national interest groups representing local government; 'spillover coalitions' and 'professional-bureaucratic complexes' that serve to undermine the distinctive political authority of elected representatives at the subnational and, in particular, the local level. However, such a change has clearly not occurred to the same degree in France and Italy — and possibly Spain — as it appears to have done in Scandinavia and Britain. Consequently, if this line of argument is correct, the conditions under which local politics either retained or lost national political significance become crucial to our understanding of the causes of different patterns of central–local relations. Local government has national political significance when there exists a firm pillar of effective support at the national level for the expression of the needs of localities, as opposed to mere 'sympathy' for local government as a whole.

Such support continues to exist in France, Italy and Spain, although it has been eroded, if indeed it ever existed, in both Scandinavia and Britain. By contrast, in North Europe, the centre appears to have been far more willing to trust local government with service delivery — at least until recently — leaving them relatively free to determine service levels once an overall framework for the service had been established. Such trust does not seem to have developed in the South European countries, with the result that localities had fewer functions and more detailed control exerted over them. In recent years, however, these contrasting patterns seem to have been reversed: in South Europe, despite fiscal stress, central government has been devolving functions to subnational level, and is beginning to distance itself from the details of the locality, if not the region. In northern Europe, despite some earlier decentralization, patterns of enhanced central control over local government have emerged, which have begun to involve the centre far more in the details of the locality. If localities in the North have not yet developed the pillar of support at national level that would give them national political significance, they certainly occupy more of the centre's time. The evidence from Spain and France at least suggests that the reverse is true of recent decentralization moves.

Just as, in historical terms, we have seen contrasting experiences of central–local government relations in North and South Europe, so today can we see further contrasts, even if overall the systems of local government and of functional allocation, discretion and access are moving closer together. Our brief review of cultural, religious, historical and size/efficiency explanations suggests they all lack something, and that an explanation in terms of the centre's need to manage and control its local territories would be more profitable.

References

Administrationsdepartementet (1982), *Statslige forskrifter for kommunernes virkomhed del II og II*. Copenhagen: Administrations-departmentet.

Alibes, J.M. et al. (1974), *La Barcelona de Porcioles*, Barcelona: Laia.

Andersson, S., Lane, J.-E. and Westin T. (1985), 'Landstinget, sjukvardsbudgetering och politik', *Statsvetenskaplig Tidskrift*.

Archer, M.G. (1979), *Social Origins of Educational Systems*, London: Sage Publications.

Ashford, D.E. (1979), 'Territorial Politics and Equality: Decentralisation in the Modern State', *Political Studies*, 27:71-83.

Ashford, D.E. (1982), *British Dogmatism and French Pragmatism*, London: Allen and Unwin.

Association of County Councils (1980), *Review of Government Controls over Local Authorities*, London: ACC.

Becquart-Leclercq, J. (1976), *Paradoxes du Pouvoir Local*, Paris: Presses de la Fondation Nationale des Sciences Politiques.

Bentzon, K.H. (1981), *Kommunalpolitikerne*, Copenhagen: Samfundsvidens-kabeligt Forlag.

Birkinshaw, P. (1982), 'Homelessness and the Law: the Effects and Response to Legislation', *Urban Law and Policy*, 5:255-95.

Birrell, W.D. and Murie A. (1980), *Policy and Government in Northern Ireland*, Dublin: Gill and Macmillan.

Blau, P. (1974), *On the Nature of Organisation*, New York: John Wiley & Sons.

Boaden, N.T. (1971), *Urban Policy Making*, London: Cambridge University Press.

Boddy, M. (1984), 'Local Councils and the Fiscal Squeeze', in M. Boddy and C. Fudge (eds), *Local Socialism*, London: Macmillan.

Bogason, P. (1980), 'Changes in Control Patterns in the Danish Political System 1966-80', Paper presented at the ECPR joint session, Florence, March.

Bogason, P. and Zachariassen, Z. (1984), *Statslig-Kommunale Plansystemer*, Copenhagen: AKFs Forlag.

Borja, A.J. (1977), 'Urban Social Movements in Spain', in M. Harloe (ed.), *Captive Cities*, Chichester: Wiley.

Borja, A.J. et al. (1972), 'La Gran Barcelona', *CAU*, 10.

Bowman, M. and Hampton, W. (eds) (1983), *Local Democracies: A Study in Comparative Local Government*, Melbourne: Longman Cheshire.

Bruknapp, A. and Sand, P. (1985), 'Makko-et Analyseverktøy for Kommunal Økonomi', in *Økonomiske Analyser*, 5, Oslo.

Bruun, F. and Skovsgaard, C.-J. (1980), 'Self-Determinination in Denmark', *International Political Science Review*, 10: 227-44.

Bulpitt, J. (1982), 'Conservatism, Unionism and Territorial Management', in P.J. Madgwick and R. Rose (eds), *The Territorial Dimension in United Kingdom Politics*, London: Macmillan.

Bulpitt, J. (1983), *Territory and Power in the United Kingdom*, Manchester: Manchester University Press.

Carr, R. (1983), *Spain 1808-1975*, Oxford: Oxford University Press.

Casanova, A.G. (1979), *Federalismo y Autonomía: Catalunia y el Estado Español*, Barcelona: Ed. Crítica.

Castells, M. (1984), *The City and the Grassroots*, London: Edward Arnold.

Cauchi, P. (1984), 'Kommunernes beskaeftigelspolitik', in C.-J. Skovsgaard et al. (eds), *Kommunernes Service under pres*. Copenhagen: Jurist-og Økonomforbundets Forlag.

Cawson, A. and Saunders, P. (1983), 'Corporatism, Competitive Politics and Class

Struggle', in R. King (ed.), *Capital and Politics*, London: Routledge and Kegan Paul.

CEUMT (1981), *La reforma administratira municipal de Barcelona*, No 34:5–10.

CEUMT (1983), *Manual de Formación Municipal*, 2nd edn, Barcelona: Centre d'Estudis Urbanistica.

CEUMT (1984), 'Las Decentralization a debate', *CEUMT*, Nos 81–2.

Chester, D.N. (1951), *Central and Local Government*, London: Macmillan.

Christensen, J. (1984), 'Kommunernes landsforening: Interesseorganisation og serviceorgan', in P.-E. Mouritzen and T. Jensen (eds), *Samspillet mellem staten og kommunerne*, Copenhagen: Jurist og Økonomforbundets Forlag.

Clarke, J.J. (1939), *The Local Government System of the United Kingdom*, 12th edn, London: Pitman.

Clavero Arevalo, M. (1983), *España, desde el Centralismo a las Autonomias*, Madrid: Ed. Planeta.

Cockburn, C. (1977), *The Local State*, London: Pluto Press.

Comision de Expertos (1982), 'Informe sobre la financión de las Autonomías', in J. Tornos (ed.), *Legislación sobre Comunidades Autonomas*, vol. 1, Madrid: Ed. Tecnos.

Crozier, M. (1964), *The Bureaucratic Phenomenon*, London: Tavistock.

Crozier, M. et al. (1974), *Où va l'administration française?* Editions des Organisations, Paris.

Damgaard, E. (1977), *Folketinget under forandring*, Copenhagen: Samfundsviden-skabeligt Forlag.

Danish Ministry of Housing (1978), *Redegørelse om by-og boligforbedring*, Copenhagen: Ministry of Housing.

Dearlove, J. (1973), *The Politics of Policy in Local Government*, London: Cambridge University Press.

Dearlove, J. (1979), *The Reorganisation of British Local Government*, London: Cambridge University Press.

Dilling-Hansen, M. (1984), 'Udviklingen i de kommunale budgetter 1978–83', in C.J. Skovsgaard et al. (eds), *Kommunernes Service under pres*, Copenhagen: Jurist- og Økonomforbundets Forlag.

Dilling-Hansen, M. et al. (1985), *Regional ulighed*. Aarhus: University of Aarhus (mimeo).

Doig, A.A. (1984), *Corruption and Misconduct in Contemporary British Politics*, Harmondsworth, Mddx: Penguin.

Duclaud-Williams, R. (1978), *The Politics of Housing in Britain and France*, London: Heinemann.

Dunleavy, P. (1981a), 'Professional Policy Change: Notes Towards a Model of Ideological Corporatism', *Public Administration Bulletin*, 36:3–16.

Dunleavy, P. (1981b), *The Politics of Mass Housing in Britain 1945–1975*, Oxford, Clarendon Press.

Dunleavy, P. (1984), 'The Limits to Local Government', in M. Boddy and C. Fudge (eds), *Local Socialism*, London: Macmillan.

English, J. (ed.) (1981), *The Future of Council Housing*, London: Croom Helm.

Erskine, A. (1984), 'Housing Benefits: Some Preliminary Comments', *Critical Social Policy*, 9:99–105.

Eurostat (1983), *General Government Accounts and Statistics 1970–1981*, Luxembourg: Eurostat.

Expertgruppen för offentlig ekonomi (1983), *Generellt statsbidrag till kommuner*, Stockholm: Finansdepartementet (DsFi 1983:26).

Fevolden, T. and Sørensen, R. (1983), 'Spillet om Skatteutjamningen', *Tidsskrift for Samfunnsforskning*, 24:59–76.

Finer, H. (1950), *English Local Government*, London: Methuen.
Flora, P. and Alber, J. (1981), 'Modernisation, Democratisation and the Development of Welfare States in Europe', in P. Flora and A.J. Heidenheimer (eds), *The Development of Welfare States in Europe and America*, New Brunswick: Transaction Books.
Folketinget (1984), Copenhagen: Folketingets Praesidium.
Friisberg, J. (1984), 'Statens styring af kommunernes: budgetsamarbejdet', in P. Mouritzen et al. (eds), *Samspillet mellem staten og kommunerne*, Copenhagen: Jurist- og Økonomforbundets Forlag.
Garcia de Enterria, E. (1972), *La administracion española*, Madrid: Ed. Alianza.
Geijer, C.W., Lindquist, U. and Nilsson, J. (1980), *Lokala Organ i Kommunerna*, Stockholm: Liber.
Gidlund, J. (1983), *Kommunal självstyrelse i fövandling*, Stockholm: Liber.
von Gneist, R. (1981), *History of the English Constitution*, London: Clowes.
Goldsmith, M. (1983), 'The Politics of Planning', in M.J. Bruton (ed.), *The Spirit and Purpose of Planning*, London: Hutchinson.
Goldsmith, M. and Newton, K. (1984), 'Central–Local Government Relations: The Irresistible Rise of Centralised Power', in H. Berrington (ed.), *Change in British Politics*, London: Frank Cass.
Goldsmith, M. (1985), 'Managing the Periphery in a Period of Fiscal Stress', in M. Goldsmith (ed.), *New Research in Central–Local Relations*, Farnborough: Gower.
Greenwood, R. (1981), 'Fiscal Pressure and Local Government in England and Wales', in *Big Government in Hard Times*, Oxford: Martin Robertson.
Greenwood, R. (1982), 'Pressures from Whitehall', in R. Rose and E. Page (eds), *Fiscal Stress in Cities*, London: Cambridge University Press.
Gremion, P. (1970), Introduction a une étude du système politico-ádministratif local, *Sociologie du Travail*, 1:51–73.
Griffith, E.S. (1927), *The Development of Modern City Government*, 2 vols, Oxford: Clarendon Press.
Griffith, J.A.G. (1966), *Central Departments and Local Authorities*, London: Allen and Unwin.
Gustafsson, A. (1984), *Local Government in Sweden*, Stockholm: The Swedish Institute.
Gustafsson, G. (1980), *Local Government Reform in Sweden*, Umea: Gleerup.
Gutchen, H. (1961), 'Local Government Improvements and Centralisation in Nineteenth Century England', *Historical Journal*, 4.
Gyford, J. and James, M. (1983), *National Parties and Local Politics*, London: Allen and Unwin.
Haider, D.H. (1974), *When Governments Come to Washington*, New York: Free Press.
Harder, E. (1973), *Local Government in Denmark*, Copenhagen: Det Danske Selskab.
Harris, G.M. (1933), *Local Government in Many Lands*, London: D.S. King.
Heclo, H. (1981), 'Towards a New Welfare State', in Flora P. and A. Heidenheimer (eds), *The Development of Welfare States in Europe and America*, New Brunswick: Transaction Books.
Hellners, T. (1983), *Förvaltningslagen*, Stockholm: Liber.
Herlitz, N. (1928), *Grunddragen av Det Svenska Statsskickets Historia*, Stockholm: Norstedts.
Hintze, O. (1962) 'Staatenbildung und Kommunalverwaltung', in O. Hintze, *Staat und Verfassung Gesammelte Abhandlungen zur Allgemeinen Verfassungsgeschichte*, Göttingen: Vandenhoeck & Ruprecht.
Hogwood, B.W. and Keating, M.J. (eds) (1982), *Regional Government in England*, Oxford: Clarendon Press.

INLOGOV (1983), 'Mandatory and Discretionary Provisions in Local Government', Birmingham: Institute of Local Government Studies, mimeo.

Johansson, L. (1976), 'Landstingskommunera: organisation, beslutsprocess och service-eutbud', doctoral dissertation, Lund: University of Lund, Department of Political Science.

Johansson, L. (1982), *Kommunal Servicevariation*, Stockholm: Liber.

Keating, M., Midwinter, A. and Taylor, P. (1983), 'Excessive and Unreasonable: The Politics of the Scottish Hit List', *Political Studies*, 31 (3), September 1983: 394–417.

Keith-Lucas, B. (1977), *English Local Government in the 19th and 20th Centuries*, London: Historical Association monographs no. 90.

Kelsen, H. (1949), *General Theory of Law and State*, Cambridge, Mass: Harvard University Press.

Kesselman, M. (1967), *The Ambiguous Consensus*, New York: Knopf.

King, A. (1984), *Fiscal Tiers. The Economics of Multi-Level Government*, London: Allen and Unwin.

Kjellberg, F. (1985), 'Local Government Reorganisation and the Welfare State', *Journal of Public Policy*, 5:215–40.

Kjellberg, F. and Myhren, K. (1975), 'The Development of Norwegian Municipal Policy. From Laissez-Faire to Redistribution', Paper prepared for the International Political Science Association, Edinburgh, September.

Kobielski, J. (1974), *L'Influence de la Structure des Communes Urbaines sur leurs Défenses de Fonctionnement*, Rennes: Université de Rennes, Laboratoire d'Economie des Villes et des Collectivités.

Kochen, M. and Deutsch, K.W. (1980), *Decentralization*, Cambridge, Mass: Oelge-schlager, Gunn and Hain.

Laffin, M. (1982), 'Professionalism in the Central–Local Government·Relationship', London: Tavistock Institute, mimeo.

Lane, J-E. and Westin, T. (1983), 'Landstingens byrakratisering', *Ekonomisk Debatt*, 6.

Lane, J-E. and Magnusson, T. (1982), 'Kommunsammanläggning och kommunala kostnader', *Tvärsnitt*, 4.

Lane, J-E., Magnusson, T. and Westlund, A. (1982), 'Kommunernas byrakratisering', *Tvärsnitt*, 2.

Leather, P. (1983), 'Housing (Dis?)investment Programmes', *Policy and Politics*, 11:215–29.

Lee, J.M. (1962), *Social Leaders and Public Persons*, Oxford: Clarendon Press.

Leijon, S., Lundin, R.A. and Persson, U. (1984), *Förvaltandets Förändring*, Lund: Doxa.

Lemarchand, R. and Eisenstadt, S.N. (eds) (1981), *Political Clientelism, Patronage and Development*, Beverly Hills: Sage Publications.

Lindquist, U. (1982), *Kommunala befogenheter*, Stockholm: Liber.

Lipsky, M. (1979), *Street Level Bureaucracy*, New York: Russell Sage Foundation.

Machado, S.M. (1982), *Derecho Public de las Comunidades Autónomas*, Vol. I, Madrid: Ed. Civitas.

Mackenzie, W.J.M. (1951), 'The Conventions of Local Government', *Public Administration*, 29:345–56.

Mackenzie, W.J.M. (1954), 'Local Government in Parliament', *Public Administration*, 32:409–23.

Madsen, S.H. (1984), 'Serviceydelser pa folkeskoleormradet', in C.-J. Skovsgaard (ed.), *Kommunernes Service under pres*, Copenhagen: Jurist- og Økonomforbundets Forlag.

Magnusson, T. and Lane, J-E. (1985), 'Kommunala VA-kostnader och system'. Research report 1985:8, Umea: University of Umea, Department of Political Science.

References 173

Medhurst, K. (1973), *Government in Spain*, New York: Pergamon.
Mény, Y. (1974), *Centralisation et Decentralisation dans le Débat Politique Français*, Paris: Librairie Générale de Droit et de Jurisprudence.'
Mény, Y. (ed.) (1982), *Dix Ans de Régionalisation en Europe*, Paris: Cujas.
Mény, Y. (1983), 'Permanence and Change: The Relations Between Central and Local Government in France', *Government and Policy*, 1:17–28.
Mouritzen, P.-E. (1982), 'Local Resource Allocation: Partisan Politics or Sector Politics?', Odense: University of Odense, mimeo.
Mouritzen, P.-E. (1984), 'Modeller af samspillet mellem staten og kommunerne', in P.-E. Mouritzen and T. Jensen (eds), *Samspillet mellem staton og kommunerne*, Copenhagen: Jurist- og Økonomenforbundets Forlag.
Murray, R. (1980), *Kommunal Service*, Stockholm: Liber.
Newton, K. and Sharpe, L.J. (1984), *Does Politics Matter?* Oxford: Clarendon Press.
Olander, L.O. (1984), *Staten, kommunerna coh servicen*. Statkommunberedningen. Stockholm: Civildepartementet (DsC 1984:5).
Ostre, S. (1984), *Kommunal Økonomikk*, Oslo: Universitetsforlaget.
Page, E.C. (1981), 'Grant Consolidation and the Development of Intergovernmental Relations in Britain and the United States', *Politics*, 1.
Page, E.C. (1982), 'Central Government Instruments of Influence upon Services Delivered by Local Authorities', Glasgow: University of Strathclyde, unpublished PhD thesis.
Page, E.C. (1983), 'Laws and Orders in Central–Local Government Relations', Glasgow: University of Strathclyde Studies in Public Policy, No. 106.
Picard, L.A. (1983), 'Decentralisation, Recentralisation and Steering Mechanisms: Paradoxes of Local Government in Denmark', *Polity*, 4:536–54.
Pliatzky, L. (1980), *Getting and Spending*, Oxford: Blackwell.
Redlich, J. and Hirst, F.W. (1958), *The History of Local Government in England*, London: Macmillan.
Regan, D.E. (1966), 'The Police Service: An Extreme Example of Central Control over Local Authority Staff', *Public Law*, Spring:3–34.
Rhodes, G. (1976), 'Local Government Finance 1918–1966', in Committee of Inquiry into Local Government Finance, *Report. Appendix 6*, London: HMSO.
Rhodes, G. (1981), *Inspectorates in British Government*, London: Allen and Unwin.
Rhodes, R. (1986), *The National World of Local Government*, London: Allen and Unwin.
Richardson, J.J. (ed.) (1982), *Policy Styles in Western Europe*, London: Allen and Unwin.
Robson, W.A. (1925), *The District Auditor. An Old Menace in a New Guise*. Fabian Tract no. 214, London: Fabian Society.
Rokkan, S. (1970), *Citizens, Electors, Parties*, Oslo: Universitetsforlaget.
Rose, R. (1982), *Understanding the United Kingdom*, London: Longman.
Rose, R. (1985a), 'The Programme Approach to the Growth of Government', *British Journal of Political Science*, 15:1–26.
Rose, R. (1985b), *Public Employment in Western Nations*. London: Cambridge University Press.
Rose, R. and Peters, B.G. (1978), *Can Government Go Bankrupt?* London: Macmillan.
Rowat, D.C. (ed.) (1980), *International Handbook on Local Government Reorganisation: Contemporary Developments*, London: Aldwych Press.
Rush, M. (1969), *The Selection of Parliamentary Candidates*, London: Nelson.
Saunders, P. (1984), 'Rethinking Local Politics', in M. Boddy and C. Fudge (eds), *Local Socialism*, London: Macmillan.

Scarrow, H. (1971), 'Policy Pressures by British Local Government: the Case of Regulation in the 'Public Interest' ', *Comparative Politics*, 4:1–28.

Schulz, M. (1948), 'The Control of Local Authority Borrowing by the Central Government', in C.H. Wilson (ed.), *Essays in Local Government*, Oxford: Blackwell.

Sharpe, L.J. (1978), 'Reforming the Grass Roots: An Alternative Analysis', in A.H. Halsey (ed.), *Policy and Politics*, London: Macmillan.

Sharpe, L.J. (1981), 'The Failure of Local Government Modernisation in Britain: A Critique of Functionalism', *Canadian Public Administration*, 24:92–115.

Sharpe, L.J. (1982), 'Labour and the Geography of Inequality: a Puzzle', in D. Kavanagh (ed.), *The Politics of the Labour Party*, London: Allen and Unwin.

Sharpe, L.J. (1984), 'Functional Allocation in the Welfare State', *Local Government Studies*, 10:27–45.

Skovsgaard, C.-J. (1984), 'Strategies for Centralisation', paper prepared for central–local government relations conference, Nuffield College, January.

Smallwood, F. (1965), *Greater London: The Politics of Metropolitan Reform*, New York: Bobbs Merrill.

Smith, B.C. (1985), *Decentralisation*, London: Allen and Unwin.

Stanyer, J. (1976), *Understanding Local Government*, Glasgow: Fontana.

Stat-Kommunbewredningen (1984), *Försök med ökad kommunal självstyrelse*, Stockholm: Civildepartementet (DsC 1984:1).

Stat-kommunbewredningen (1984), *Statlig reglering av kommunal verksamhet*, Stockholm: Civildepartementet (DsC 1984:2).

Strömberg, L., Norell, P.-O. (1982), *Kommunalförvaltningen*, Stockholm: Liber.

Swann, B. (1972), 'Local Initiative and Central Control: the Insulin Decision', *Policy and Politics*, 1:55–63.

Tarrow, S. (1977), *Between Center and Periphery. Grassroots Politicians in Italy and France*, New Haven: Yale University Press.

Temime, E., Broder, A. and Chastagnaret, G. (1982), *Historia de la Espaia Contemporanea*, Barcelona: Ed. Ariel.

de Teran, F. (1986), *Planeamento urbano en la Espaia Contemporanea*, 2nd edn, Madrid: Ed. Alianza.

Thoenig, J.-C. (1973), *L'Ere des Technocrates*, Paris: Editions d'Organisation.

Thoenig, J.-C. (1980), 'Local Subsidies in the Third Republic', in D.E. Ashford (ed.), *Financing Local Government in the Welfare State*, London: Croom Helm.

Uribarri, J.A. (1978), *Municipio, Elecciones y Vecinos*, Madrid: Ed. de la Torre.

Vandelli, L. (1982), *El ordenamiento Español de las Communidades Autónomas*. Madrid: IEAL.

Vaughan, M. and Archer, M.S. (1971), *Special Conflict and Educational Change in England and France 1789–1848*, London: Cambridge University Press.

Villadsen, S. (1984), 'Partierne i lokalpolitikken', Copenhagen: Institute of Political Studies, mimeo.

Webb, S. (1911), *Grants in Aid: A Criticism and a Proposal*, London: Longman Green.

Wiberg, S. (ed.) (1985), *Ledarskapets förnyelse*, Lund: Doxa.

Worms, J.-P. (1966), 'Le Préfet et ses Notables', *Sociologie du Travail*, 3:249–75.

Wynn, M. (1984), 'Spain', in M. Wynn (ed.), *Planning and Urban Growth in Southern Europe*, London: Mansell.

Young, K. (1984), 'Governing Greater London', *Political Quarterly*, 55:256–72.

Index

In the following index, 'local government' is abbreviated to 'l.g.'

Notes on contributors

Peter Bogason is Associate Professor at the University of Copenhagen, Institute of Political Studies.

Thomas Clegg researches at the London School of Economics.

Trond Fevolden is Deputy Director at the Ministry of Local Government and Labour in Oslo.

Michael Goldsmith is Professor of Government and Politics at the University of Salford.

Jan-Erik Lane is Professor of Public Administration at the University of Umeå.

Tage Magnusson researches at the Department of Political Science, University of Umea, Sweden.

Yves Mény is Professor of Politics at the University of Paris II.

Edward Page is Lecturer in Politics at the University of Hull.

Enzo Sanantonio researches at the Institute of Regional Studies, Rome.

Rune Sørensen is Associate Professor at the Department of Political Science, University of Oslo.